DID THE RIGHT

DID THE RIGHT SPERM WIN?

Vinette Hoffman-Jackson

YOUCAXTON PUBLICATIONS

OXFORD & SHREWSBURY

ISBN 978-191117-512-4

Printed and bound in Great Britain.
Published by YouCaxton Publications 2016

Author photograph by Michael Gnahoua.

Contents

INTRODUCTION

This book comprises thirty inspiring short stories, poems and self-reflections written to stimulate thought and inspire action towards an improved life. The book is based on my personal experiences and observations and was written to complement my journey to become a motivational speaker.

My life does not fulfil the stereotype of what a perfect life should look like but I am grateful that I have now reached a level of consciousness and spirituality that has helped me to see beyond the physical or literal level of most of life's little unexpected curve balls.

While not all my stories may resonate with everyone, I can guarantee that at least one will undoubtedly appeal to you. Read each chapter to see how many of life's simple events or occurrences are designed to give you a message. There are no accidents. The people you meet, the places you travel and the things that are done to you are all for a reason. They happened to either convey a message or direct your path. Ultimately, only our reaction to each of these will determine the next chapter of your life.

Try and find the silver lining in every cloud. There is always one.

DEDICATION

This book is dedicated firstly to God, my continued source of strength. I can do all things through Christ who strengthens me.

To my three sons Matthew, Jonathan and Ethan. You are the reasons I get out of bed each morning. Thank you for always believing in Mommy. I love you.

Special thank you to the following people who have kept me going even when I felt like quitting

- Teslyn Dawkins
- Debrah Kaye Dawkins
- Shirlette Dawkins
- Orlando Dawkins
- Charles Seanla

And of course to all the Pharaohs in my life: I am eternally grateful for the pain and obstacles you have caused or created. It made me a stronger and more determined woman and gave me the motivation to push harder towards success.

CHAPTER 1

The Psychic

She walked in and immediately I was drawn to her. There was just something about her. An aura, the way she dressed, her eyes, I could not really say but there was just something about her that was different. I do not know how to describe it; it was like a hundred people walking safely past a dog and he just chooses one person to bite. Why that one? Did they give off a certain smell or look a certain way?

She did not look out of place or odd, in fact she looked like any ordinary person in the café. But a strong emotion came over me and I had absolutely no explanation whatsoever. I just did not know what to feel or how to act. Should I should laugh, cry, hate, love … what?

So in the end I settled on disgust!

I started looking around, just to catch someone's attention, anyone; just to establish eye contact and to validate that what I was seeing and feeling was shared by another human being. I kept darting my eyes around the room trying to find that one person who was looking in the same direction. I swivelled my head in every direction possible and so quickly

I almost felt dizzy. I even half stood up, holding onto the arms of my chair to balance myself, to make sure I could scan the entire room.

About a minute later my frantic search was rewarded. I finally found who I had been searching for, a kindred spirit. We did not need words because her expression said it all. We briefly acknowledged each other through a slight nod of the head then returned our gaze to our mutual object of derision. With matching scowls we looked the other girl up and down, from the top of her head to the soles of her feet. Without reason I hated her long red locks and dark brown eyes.

She must have felt our eyes so she slowly turned to face me and, seeing my expression, immediately dropped her gaze and walked briskly from the café.

I looked back at my new found partner in disgust and we smirked, shook our heads from side to side and with a tiny shrug of the shoulder went about our day without even an introduction. It was not needed.

A few hours later I had forgotten about the stranger and the girl with the red hair and deep brown eyes; we were immersed in our own worlds once again.

§

'No!' I protested, 'I can't stand these people, they are complete rip-offs.' My plea fell on deaf ears as my best friend pushed me towards the open tent. I wish I had pretended to be sick instead of being dragged to the town's annual travelling fair.

Madame Crystal the sign read on the entrance to the tent. *Will read your life and tell your future.* Yeah right! 'Okay, okay, let's see what Madame Crystal has to say about me' I rolled my eyes and entered the dimly lit tent.

The scent of candles and some other exotic ointments greeted us as we entered. There she sat, the wise old sage. I could literally laugh out loud.

'Sit down.' She beckoned to the empty chair placed in front of an old ball that looked like crystal but I would guess was just cheap glass.

I sat down.

'Place your hand on the crystal ball please,' she commanded in one of these voices that I am sure they learn at Crystal Ball College. I smiled at my own joke.

I obliged. This was followed by a series of 'hmmmm,' 'aaaaah,' 'aha,' and various other utterances. Finally she spoke to me in English. 'You're very, very special.'

I wished she would tell me something I did not know.

'You have the gift of foresight,' she continued, 'although you don't know it.' She smiled and looked at me and held my gaze in a way that caused me to shift uncomfortably in my seat and look away. 'Do you ever get a strong feeling about someone without actually knowing the person?'

I stopped smirking. 'Y-y-yes,' I stuttered. 'Just recently I was in a coffee shop ...' I stopped mid-sentence.

'Go on,' she encouraged.

My old cynicism had returned. 'You are the psychic,' I replied. 'Why don't you tell me what happened?'

She smiled slowly and I leaned forward, taking a keen interest in what she had to say.

'Ah yes,' she continued, 'there are some people who can see what others cannot see. They see through the eyes of a higher order. You might sometimes hate a person for no apparent reason because you can see beyond their current situation. You can see the greatness that lies beneath and it threatens your superiority. When this happens it's so overwhelming you may not know how to feel or how to act. Whether you should laugh, cry, hate or love.'

Without a word I got up and ran ...

I could hear my friend shouting 'wait, wait' as I ran home.

I could still see that girl in the café, the one I felt utter disgust for. Could crystal-ball granny be right?

§

After three years I finally got my promotion. I was so keen to create a correct first impression, I walked into the conference room and greeted the room of twelve with a cheery 'Good morning everyone!' As our boss entered I heard myself exclaiming 'I like your hair boss!' and cringed as soon as the kiss-up words left my lips.

'Thank you,' she replied as she ran her slender fingers through her long red locks. Her brown eyes were mesmerising and smiling.

Final Comments

There will always be people you come across in life who might show a strong dislike for you and some will seemingly go out of their way to destroy you. Even if you are as nice as you can be, nothing you do will change their minds. Have you ever walked into a room and suddenly turned to see someone giving you dirty looks or looking you over from head to toe and not in an admiring way? These are people you have never seen before but immediately they have decided they do not like you.

It might be that these people see the greatness in you even if you do not. They realise that there is something about you, something that makes you stand out. You do not need to speak or do anything but as you walk into a room you will be noticed. You have what is called *presence*.

Recently I worked in a company where a few people took a dislike to me for no apparent reason and, after trying several times to be liked, I finally gave up. I realised I had done nothing unkind or disrespectful to these people; they had just decided they did not like me. It could have been the shoes I wear, the car I drive, my partner, where I live or just because my name starts with a 'V'. Their feelings towards me did not require a valid reason so I gave up searching for one. I simply went about my life pushing towards my goals until I finally achieved them without the friendship or endorsement of these people. At the end of the day they were never going to help me realise my dreams even if they liked me; so it did not really matter.

It may be hard or almost impossible but try not to hate these people; they do not yet understand their psychic gifts. Use their dislike and hatred to push onwards and upwards. Keep working at your dreams and fulfil the purpose that has been in your mind from ever since you can remember. Whatever it is that you know and believe you were made to do, even if no one sees it. Keep moving towards that goal.

CHAPTER 2

The Body Clock

'Tick-tock, tick-tock!' I whispered with mirth and mischief in my voice. 'That clock is ticking. Time to get a move on, Tes!'

Tes half turned in her chair so she was no longer facing me directly. With a casual sideways glance she cast a frustrated look in my direction then continued nibbling on her scone and reading her book. 'I'm in no rush, thank you, so let that clock keep on ticking,' Tes retorted. The symbolism of the moment was not lost as I pointed to the title of the book she was now engrossed in: *Did the Right Sperm Win?*

'Really? Are you sure?' No response. 'Well I'm certainly impressed!' I continued. 'When I was told about my body clock I leapt up, ran home to my husband and starting working immediately.'

'You are disgusting, eeeeew!' Tes shrieked. 'A little bit too much information,' she added.

'What?' I asked, genuinely puzzled. 'You're really acting weird. What the hell is in those scones? I'm trying to explain that when I found out about my body clock I realised I had to move quickly. I had never heard about it before and just hearing about it at thirty-nine meant there was no time to lose. It's been five years and I can tell you, we've not gotten there yet, but not a single day has passed since I heard about my body clock when Tony and I have not been working at it. We make every minute count.'

As she sputtered at my last statement, bits of scone flew from Tes's mouth, narrowly missing my eye, but a few bits got caught in my hair. Her reaction was confusing.

She regained her composure and quietly marked the page she was reading, closed her book and readjusted in her seat so she could look directly into my eyes. 'Look here Debbie,' she glared, struggling to keep her voice low and calm. 'I don't want to hear the sordid details of your sex life. I'm your ...'

'Whoa!' I interrupted. 'What the hell are you talking about? When did I speak about my sex life?' I leaned in closer to her, conscious of a few stares we were now getting from the tables next to ours. Probably a café in the middle of June on a side street in London at midday was not the best venue for such conversation. Nevertheless we could not stop mid-way through; it had to be discussed.

'Well ah, you ah ...' Tes mumbled, searching for the right words, and reflecting on the conversation that had just taken place. 'Hmmm, body clock... ticking...Tony... at it... hmmmm?' Could she have misinterpreted the conversation? Highly unlikely she mentally concluded.

'Wait a minute,' said Tes. 'What do you mean by "going at it"?'

'Working on my dreams,' I responded, unsure if I understood her question.

'Specifically what dreams?' Tes persisted.

'The dream I've always had,' I slowly replied as if talking to someone with a delayed mental age. 'To own my own designing firm with my husband, Tony - why?'

'Ok,' she eyed me suspiciously. 'What about your body clock? What does that mean to you?'

'Glad you asked,' I replied. 'Five years ago I asked that very same question of an old lady who was sitting next to me on a train. We had just passed a billboard showing a woman carrying a briefcase in one hand and a baby in the other. Beneath the picture the slogan read "Your body clock is ticking!" I just didn't understand the advert so I turned to the nearest person, an old lady, and asked if she understood what it meant. She smiled and told me a story.'

'A long time ago when life was simpler, when black was black and white was white and when good was good and bad was bad, mankind was protected by a great wizard who was very kind. He ruled well and was loved by all. He was known fondly as "the Timekeeper". Mankind knew they would only remain alive for a certain time, and to remind each newly born human child he would give each of them a clock as a gift.

These clocks were different to the clocks we have today. These clocks had the time each child had left to live on earth down to the very second. This made life much more organised and productive as people worked and lived with the knowledge of how much time they had left.

'Then one day there was a falling out amongst the other great wizards. One wizard felt life lacked spontaneity and had become boring as everyone knew the moment they would all die and other wizards supported this new theory. All the wizards gathered together to find a solution to the problem raised as was customary when there was a disagreement amongst them. The disgruntled wizard proposed that all body clocks should be abolished and mankind should have no reminder of how much time they have left; others preferred the current system. A few even thought that only the wealthy should have the privilege of knowing when their time was up. They argued for many months but could never resolve their issues, and so they decided to go their own separate ways. They all chose to go to different planets where each would rule alone so there would be no more disagreements. The great wizard wanted to be left on earth but the others felt that this gave him an unfair advantage so in the end he had to move to a new planet as well. But the great wizard was so in love with mankind that he secretly left each human being with a timer inside.'

Then she stopped talking. I looked outside and realised I had already passed my stop, but I still wanted to hear more. So I gently asked, 'A timer? Counting down?'

She smiled, looked at me and said, 'Sssh!'

I glanced around not sure what I was looking for. 'Sssh, listen,' she said. 'What do you hear?'

'People talking,' I replied.

'No, closer,' she whispered with a hint of impatience.

'The train?' I nervously replied.

'Closer.'

'You talking.'

'Closer.'

As I became a bit freaked out my breath became sharper and after a while I could actually hear my own breathing. I listened for about a minute and then the realisation hit. My countdown body clock!

'It's each breath I take,' I shouted.

She smiled.

Suddenly I became more conscious that I was breathing rapidly and immediately made an effort to think positive happy thoughts. My breathing slowed right down.

'He left our lungs to work as a timer,' she continued. 'Each breath we take means we have less time left. Each intake is usually about one second; and each time we exhale is another second. Whenever anyone gets angry or upset they use up a lot of their time quickly but when they're calm and smiling it slows time down. The clock does not tell you the exact time it will stop but acts as a count-down reminder.'

The train pulled to a stop. 'Tick-tock,' the old woman whispered and was off!

§

Tes's eyes were as big as two saucers, 'Debbie!' she exclaimed, 'each complete breath, normal breathing really is about two seconds. My God, my countdown timer is my body clock!'

She looked at me with new realisation and without another word Tes grabbed her book, shoved the last piece of scone into her mouth and was off sending napkins and a few utensils flying.

'Tick-tock! Tick-tock!' I whispered and smiled.

Final Comments

How much time do you have left on your body clock? To be honest, the answer is really not important, what is important is what you do with whatever time you have left.

They say if you want to hide something, the best place to hide it is in full view of everyone. Wherever you are right now reading this book, I guarantee you that ninety-nine per cent of you will have some sort of device that tells the time or you can get to one within a few steps. It may be a mobile phone, computer, car dashboard, watch or a clock on a wall; but with so many items recoding the passage of time, how many take note of time actually passing?

When you check that text message or make that call do you see the time? Most people do not. You simply change the screen without even looking.

Time is elusive and never stops moving even if you do. Controversially, since time is in perpetual motion, contrary to widely held beliefs there is no past, present and future; there is only the past and the future. The present exists so briefly that it can be ignored. Puzzled? Let me explain: up until this point all that you have read is in the past. The thoughts that just flashed across your mind are already in the past. In fact by the time you say, do or think anything they are all in the past. You need to live for the future by starting to live now. Your choices and decisions made in the now will determine who you are in the future.

What are you waiting for?

Well most people wait on a specific moment to start something important in their lives. We wait for the New Year to start that diet, or until we have enough money to start that business, and the list goes on. Each moment delayed is a moment lost forever. The time will never be just perfect.

What are YOU waiting for?

CHAPTER 3

I Love You

With tears in his eyes, a pounding heart and a roughly packed suitcase with clothes hanging out, he stood waiting for the train. For a fleeting moment the forbidden thought entered his head as the train came into the station: just two steps and it would all be over. It would definitely ease the indescribable pain he felt in his heart and in his soul. His throat was parched, partly due to the shouting, screaming and pleading he had been doing for the past few days and the many tears he had shed. With a vacant stare he slowly lifted his old, battered suitcase and dragged his body, shoulders drooping and almost in a complete daze, towards the open train doors. He scoured the train carriage to find an empty seat near the window. He did not want to be disturbed from his thoughts; he wanted no uninvited chatting or, even worse, happy people to distract him from the sorrow he was feeling. He felt almost masochistic; the pain reminded him that he was alive and offered despondence and hope in the same moment. He would survive but for now he just wanted to grieve in peace.

He heard a distant whistle and felt a slight jolt as the train rolled slowly out of the station and into the open countryside. Realising he was alone he allowed himself the luxury of a low moan. He tried to cry but no sound or tears came; he had exhausted his supply.

Slowly his thoughts drifted back to just five months ago. He could still smell her, feel her, taste her as if it was yesterday. He closed his eyes and visualised the scene and a smile came gently to his face.

§

Standing on the pier he held her and tenderly gazed into her brown eyes. He felt as if the world was spinning and he was drowning in her eyes. Tenderly he caressed her cheek with the back of his hand and gently whispered, 'I love you!'

She responded by squeezing him tightly against her body, smiled and said, 'I love you too!'

They shared a kiss and thought themselves lucky to find their soul mate, knowing that they would be together for a lifetime. Hand in hand and with his arm resting on her shoulder, they walked slowly.

'No!' he cried, the sound of his own voice roughly dragging him back to his current reality.

§

It was too much and he shook his head to escape the movie being played in his mind. He started thinking: what do those words mean - 'I love you'? Clearly it meant different things to different people. If only he had known five months ago.

Final Comments

When a person says 'I love you', what does it mean? Many times people say these three words and at the time they mean it to their core but everyone says these words based on their limited understanding.

One needs to understand that different people use these words in different contexts. One person based on his/her culture, past experiences, knowledge *et cetera* may have concluded that love means being able to financially provide for one's family; another person's understanding of love may mean total loyalty and commitment, being with the person day and night and money does not matter.

Then let's say these two people, person A and person B, meet and find themselves physically attracted to each other. Both now confess their undying love for each other. In truth, neither has lied because they both know they love each other.

The mistake here is that neither has bothered to explain or define what love means to them to the other; they rely on the assumption that they somehow have the same understanding of the concept of love. So when, months or years down the line, person A starts cheating or acting in an uncaring way but insists he still loves person B, they inevitably cannot understand how this could be. But it is simply because the concept of love means different things to different people. Person A is still providing for his family and working hard to make sure his family is financially secure; he believes he is doing exactly what he promised. The fact that he is sleeping around is irrelevant as he never promised to be faithful. Person B also believes they are not at fault because they are always available and one hundred percent loyal and committed just like they had promised to be. So both parties blame the other, when in truth neither is wrong.

One must also understand that as one grows and experiences new things in life, definitions and ideas about love will also change. At twenty 'I love you' meant I could call you at any time, day or night. It meant I will meet your parents, friends, cousins and pets and we could make passionate love all night.

At forty years old the definition change to include a key to your apartment, access to phones, emails and your twitter account. I no longer needed to meet everyone in your life and making love was now twice weekly.

At sixty I was just satisfied with companionship and a great sense of humour.

This meant my partner and I remained together. He grew with me; otherwise at each stage I would have needed to look for someone different as my definition changed.

Remember, even God in his infinite wisdom clearly defines his love. Why should mere men not follow his example?

In 1 Corinthians 13 vs 4-7, God clearly explain what loves mean to him:

- Love suffereth long, and is kind; Love envieth not; Love vaunteth not itself, is not puffed up,
- Doth not behave itself unseemly, seeketh not her own, is not easily provoked, thinketh no evil;
- Rejoiceth not in iniquity, but rejoiceth in the truth;
- Beareth all things, believeth all things, hopeth all things, endureth all things.

God goes on to say in John 3 vs 16: 'God so loved the world that he gave his only begotten son.' This clearly explains exactly what type of sacrifice he will make to prove his love for us.

So the next time you fall in love make sure each party has a very clear definition of exactly what love means. It may save a whole lot of time and heartache.

CHAPTER 4

Life is Not Fair!

Four boys stood in front of their father with dread,
As they waited in line to hear what would be said.

They each knew very little of the world outside,
And to find out, each would have to decide,
to step out of their comfort zone
And face life's challenges all alone.

The father came in and looked at each of his sons
and quietly prayed, his advice they would understand.

'My sons you have lived a very sheltered life.
Free from war, hurt or strife.
You have never seen the world as it truly is;
with all its joys and hidden ills.
But today as you each depart from this place,
I'll give you my best piece of advice, just in case.
This world may or may not care,
but always remember, *Life is not fair!*'

So off they each went with his sage advice.
Each to wander and live their own lives.

The first went off and in a cabin hid,
and all his dreams he never did.

The second decided to fight for it all,
got lost and ended up missing his true call.

The third worked the hardest to rectify what his father
had said,
But fate was against him and in a year he was dead.

Then I was left alone, all by myself,
to find my fame and discover my wealth.
I loved and lost and loved again
I enjoyed the victories and learnt from the pain.
I lived my life with great cunning and dare,
and all because I remembered that father had said
'Life is not fear!'

Final Comments

I am sure every one of us has heard, used or experienced
the meaning of the phrase 'life is not fair'. We use this phrase

usually when we are at the negative end of some circumstance or situation in our lives. Most of us have grown up hearing this familiar phrase and because of it many people have stopped trying - and some never tried at all because they had that phrase firmly embedded in their psyche. For some this phrase is a crutch or excuse for not pushing through life's disappointments and setbacks; they accept the fact and usually feel they are the ones whom life has treated unfairly.

Somehow we rarely hear this phrase from the other end, when things are going well. I suppose when things are going well it really does not matter if life is fair or not because, even if it is not, no one will complain.

But where did this phrase originate? Who said it and why? It would be interesting to find out.

One perspective that we have not examined is the possibility of a mistake in either the translation, diction or recording of this simple but profound statement. 'Life is not fair' is stating a fact that is blatantly obvious; it is an impossibility for life to be fair. We are all different, with different backgrounds, culture and outlook and belief systems, so fairness will always mean different things to different people.

However, if we translate the statement to mean 'life is not FEAR' then it is a whole new game. Now it is all about everyone facing life head on, meeting our challenges without the usual tentative reservations that limit our excellence and reduce many of life's experiences that would have made us better people; helped us to fulfil those dreams that never came to fruition.

I once read a question that asked 'What would you do, if you knew you could not fail?' Using the maxim 'Life is not fear' would make this question a lot easier to answer. We would simply do all that we can do, because fear had been reduced or eliminated.

It is time to adopt the new translation and start to chase your dreams a little bit harder, to take greater risks. When life meets you with setbacks and disappointments do not just accept it, keep pushing through the hurt and the pain knowing no fear.

Start living with the new phrase 'Life is not fear!'

CHAPTER 5

Live Life Like a FTSE 500 Company

What makes some companies successful while others fail? Depending on who you ask, you will get a range of viewpoints, each expressed with undeniable conviction.

Whatever the reason or reasons, no one can deny the need for 'good, reliable and trustworthy' employees. Without the right employees the best vision, strategic planning, financial security all become useless. The wrong person in a job can cause a company to go into liquidation, become bankrupt and eventually cease to exist.

Most successful companies employ similar types of people, albeit with different titles but the job descriptions are pretty similar.

The main roles in successful companies are as follows:

Chief Executive Officer, CEO

The CEO has responsibility for the overall success of an entire organization. The CEO has the ultimate authority to make final decisions for an organization.

The Marketing Manager

The marketing manager's main duty is to help promote a positive image to customers. It is all about selling the company to increase the customer base. Marketing is an ongoing process to establish the brand. It is said that Bentley do not need to advertise because they have established their brand and made it synonymous to reliability, excellence and style.

Chief Financial Officer, CFO

A CFO is responsible for bringing important financial controls to a company. Those controls should include the effective management of cash flow and overhead expenses.

Like it or not, money makes the world go round. Failure to control or monitor your finances will inevitably lead to failure, regardless of the effort or work put in.

Human Resources Manager, HR

This manager will act as Chair person on disciplinary hearings and will have to do the hiring and firing.

This is a very complex and highly important role because it deals with the selection of staff, the backbone of any business.

Cleaner

A Cleaner helps with general house cleaning. Many might overlook this vital role within any successful organization. I once asked some Year 9 students, 'Who do you think have a greater impact on more people: a great neurosurgeon or a bin man?' They gave the correct answer but it was a priceless moment to see the realisation in their eyes. The truth is the neurosurgeon with all his brilliance is only important if you are ill and need his services whereas the bin man is always needed because we produce rubbish daily. If the bin man ever goes on strike, within a week he will certainly be missed.

RECEPTIONIST

A receptionist is often the first business contact a person will meet in any organization. It is an expectation of most organizations that the receptionist maintains a calm, courteous and professional demeanour at all times, regardless of the visitor's behaviour. Some personal qualities that a receptionist is expected to possess in order to do the job successfully include attentiveness, a well-groomed appearance, initiative, loyalty, maturity, respect for confidentiality and discretion, a positive attitude and dependability. At times the job may be stressful due to interaction with many different people with varying types of personalities, but it is still expected that the receptionist perform multiple tasks quickly and efficiently.

The receptionist is often the first person that employees and potential clients see, so they are always representing the company.

Operations Manager

The operations manager has to handle a lot of duties: work flow, purchases, supply, inventory management and many more, often over the course of one day.

This is the person who deals with all the day to day issues.

Final Comments

Believe it or not, your life is like a company. On a daily basis you sell yourself without realising it. You are scrutinised and assessed at work. You need to use your financial skills to budget, pay bills and save. You constantly meet new people in all walks of life.

For most people, these tasks are done without any deep thought. But what if you actually think about yourself in a different light? Try, if you can, to separate each role; know when you are required to act as a Chief Executive Officer as opposed to an Operations Manager and act as such.

Who is the CEO of your life? Who makes all the decisions and hence decides your success? Everyone needs to make sure they are in charge of their lives and that they have a strategic plan. Where are you going? What is your mission statement? What are your goals? These questions should be answered without hesitation. US motivational speaker and author Earl Nightingale says, "We can let circumstances rule us, or we can take charge and rule our lives from within".

Be open to consult with other experts in this area of management or adopt a mentor. If you are so inclined prayer and God can act in this capacity.

Who do you allow to take up a space in your life? Are they fulfilling their role and helping you to achieve your goals? If they are not you may need to fire them. Do not be afraid to ask someone to leave your life if they are preventing you from achieving your purpose on earth. This would be sinful. Learn to tactfully disengage from people who do not share the same vision.

Ensure you clean up daily. Are you hoarding physical and mental rubbish? When was the last time you threw out or donated clothes you no longer wear? Are you still thinking about that friend that hurt you many moons ago? Maybe it is time to clean up.

Be careful what the public see and in some cases use to judge you. Your attire, speech and actions help them to form an opinion of you before they see the real you. The image you are presenting should be the one you want others to see. Sometimes in life we believe we are one thing and get a rude awakening when others share how they perceive us. What message are you sending to others? "Your most important sale in life is to sell yourself to yourself" - Maxwell Maltz, American scientist.

Strive for financial stability in all you do. Remember you should work to live and not live to work. Be sensible in all financial decisions. Napoleon Hill, author of *Think and Grow Rich* says money without brains is always dangerous.

From the moment you wake up you must always be aware of your actions because they have great significance in determining your day, your week, your year - or your life. One bad decision can change the course of history.

Be aware of the role you are playing and try to live your life like a FTSE 500 company!

CHAPTER 6

I Drive My Own Car

'I AM ready!' I told my driving instructor. 'You'll see, when I get back with the certificate in my hand,' I insisted.

His wary look conveyed to me that he was not convinced in the slightest. He dryly handed me the keys and walked to the café. That was the motivation I needed.

The inspector arrived and after checking my credentials and asking a few car and road-safety questions we got into the car. I breathed deeply, whispered a word or two of prayer then checked my mirrors, exhaled, put on my indicator to indicate I was pulling out, checked again then gently moved off. So far so good, I cautiously and nervously left the examination depot and joined the world of drivers on a busy street.

After about an hour of observation and directed instructions the inspector told me to drive back to the depot. By this time I was more than comfortable so I drove straight back without any incidents.

As we drove in my driving instructor was standing in the yard with his disposable cup of coffee in hand. 'Well, how did she do mate?' he enquired with very little enthusiasm or expectation.

'She passed,' came the blunt emotionless reply as the inspector walked past, eager to get to his other driving candidates.

'Congratulations,' my instructor managed to sputter between coughs as the hurriedly drunk coffee tried to escape his windpipe.

I smiled. There is no greater satisfaction than to show people you are better than their limited expectations of you.

Final Comments

I have now been driving my own car since my early twenties and I am in my early fifties. I like the freedom it gives and I am comforted by the knowledge that I can come and go as I please.

On the few occasions I have needed to transport passengers, whether family or friends, to their chosen destinations there has been never any doubt as to who will drive; I will be the one to turn the steering wheel, step on the brake when required or push down on the accelerator if I need to speed up. I am in total control.

So why do I feel the need to write about such a trivial thing as owning a car? After all, millions if not billions own their own cars all over the globe. I started thinking about this after attending a company meeting and listening to a speech being delivered by a company executive. He was trying to motivate staff to do some extra duties for £10 per hour. His method of convincing us left much to be desired though.

Mr Waofsp began by saying we should be grateful because other organisations were just paying £5 an hour. He felt this tremendous offer was like a bonus to get us to work. It was then that the figurative penny dropped.

I drive my own car but ... I do not drive my own life. My standards of living, the car I drove, the place I resided were all dictated by the salary that I was paid by my boss. He drove my life. I had allowed people to drive my life. He was in control. I was just a passenger and he was the driver.

It gave me pause for thought. There is really no comparison between a human life and a machine designed by man is there?

Why then, do we allow people to control our lives?

Some people may immediately respond by saying, 'I control my own life,' but I would love to challenge that. Firstly, if you work for someone else you are controlled. If you live or work in rented accommodation, you are controlled.

While I agree that every one of us will be controlled at some time in our life it is our responsibility to work steadfastly to reduce this control or, at best, establish joint control.

CHAPTER 7

My Best Conversation... Ever!

Yesterday I had the best conversation ever. It was way overdue! I could not believe I had never spoken to her before but as they say: nothing happens before the right time.

I had known her for as long as I could remember but somehow I never found the right time nor reason to speak to her. As we lived in the same town I would occasionally see her in passing but never really engaged with her. I literally just did not have enough time. I was always busy with family, friends and work so I could not fit her into my busy schedule.

Occasionally though I would hear people talk about her and I would nod in agreement, or offer a word in her defence if I thought they were being too harsh. I can still remember an incident when I was hiding away in my cubby hole to escape the rat race when two of my friends walked in. As they started gossiping about her, laughing and being very unkind, I remember quietly shedding tears for her. But I was still too afraid to talk to her.

I remember people used to joke that if I spoke to her others would think I was mad and lock me away, so I dismissed the idea of ever speaking to her.

It was just by chance today as I was passing by my favourite coffee shop and having nothing planned for the day, I peeked through the front window and I caught a glimpse of her just standing there. She looked a bit older, a bit wiser but still beautiful, and I turned away quickly just to avoid her eyes.

But there was something in her eyes as she looked at me, a kind of sadness that compelled me to stare at her. We stood looking at each other before I slowly managed a smile and she smiled back. Afraid others might see me, I hurriedly nodded for her to follow and met up with her near the lake. I looked into the water and saw her reflection standing on the banks of the lake. It was quiet and secluded and there was no chance of being seen, and for the first time I spoke to her.

We talked so much. Then we laughed and cried and shared so much.

She told me how special I was. She reminded me that I am descended from kings and queens and told me how I was made for greatness. She was so passionate that I believed every word. As she spoke I could feel my shoulders straightening and I stood taller. I felt as if I could conquer the world. I tried to tell her about my many problems and to create obstacles between us but she looked deep into my eyes and firmly reminded me once again, 'You are an amazing woman, never give up!'

I could not imagine why I had never spoken to her before but speaking to her helped me to finally understand who I was.

Yesterday I finally spoke to the person who proved to be my very best friend... I finally spoke to ME!

Final Comments

When was the last time you looked into a mirror? Not just to glance at your dress or suit, fix your make up or check how you look, but really looked at yourself? Have you ever looked into your own eyes for sixty uninterrupted seconds? You should really try it. Try and look at yourself. It may feel a bit uncomfortable at first but eventually you will feel a bit more comfortable as time goes on. The urge to look away will come and you may glance away or lose focus for a while, but force yourself to do it. Get to know you.

Try talking to yourself after a while. Talk out aloud. Share your dreams, aspirations and all your plans. Say it out loud as you would if you were talking to your best friend, because you are. Remind yourself how special you are. Get to know you.

It is such a travesty when others know you before you know yourself. When you take time to get to know yourself, well, then it is easier to challenge other's views or opinions of you. When people tell you that you are no good or you are a bad person you will be able to confidently disagree and tell them who you are. Have you ever looked into a mirror fleetingly and thought you look amazing, then taken a picture only to realise the look is completely different? For most of us, we do not look deep enough to see us; we merely look on the surface and most times we do it with a pre-conceived image in our mind. So when we glance we see some of our expectations instead of the real us, but the camera never lies and only reflects what is there; thus the mirror and the camera give two different images.

Some people can sell anything from a pin to an anchor but struggle to sell themselves because they do not know the product well. They do not know their full potential and all the strength that lies inside. Talking to yourself can help you to see all the positives in yourself that you tend to forget about in your constant bid to fix whatever you perceive to be wrong with you.

Take five minutes and go and talk to you!

CHAPTER 8

Perspectives

I once taught an art class to a group of Year-Seven students. I was a substitute teacher and the work set was to draw a statue.

I placed the statue at the front of the class and arranged the students in a semi-circle so they could all see it. I told the students to sketch the statue, which was of an old man wearing a fedora hat slightly tilted to one side.

After forty-five minutes I collected the work and left it on the desk to be marked.

I was asked to cover the same class the next day and started to hand out the marked work. I happened to glance at one piece and stifled a giggle because it looked nothing like the statue that was sitting in front of me. It seemed as though I was not the only one that lacked artistic ability. Instinctively I turned over the sheet to see the mark given. 'What?!' I was so surprised that I actually spoke out loud.

Then I checked the other pieces, all the marks ranged from an A* to a B. I looked at all the drawings and only two looked anything like the statue the students were asked to draw.

This teacher clearly had just given random marks without bothering to check.

After the lesson I was still feeling a bit upset so I went to speak to the Head of Art about the marking. He came over, looked at the statue and the marks and told me, 'Mrs Jackson, It's all about perspective.' He invited me to sit in all the chairs and look at the statue again. Sure enough, every view was completely different even though it was the same statue.

In fact the drawing that I had judged to be the worst was actually the most accurate when I saw things from the child's perspective.

Final Comments

Which angle are you looking at things from? Just by changing your perspective you can give your life a whole new meaning. When faced with problems or disagreements simply trying to look at things from a different angle can save you a lot of hurt.

My grandmother used to tell me that there are three sides to every story; my side, your side and the true side. Life is always about perspectives. Often if we can only exercise a little patience to try and understand why others react in a certain way, then we would prevent a lot of arguments or fall-outs.

Nowhere is this more evident than in motor-vehicle accidents, especially the minor ones. Everyone will start placing blame on the other party because of the consequences in higher premiums and possible points on their licences if they are held responsible; no one is willing to just look at the facts and see things from the other perspective.

Try seeing things from other people's perspective. Their culture, background, socialisation or education may strongly influence how they see things and influence their reactions in given situations. Try not to judge people until you understand why they behave the way they do.

CHAPTER 9

The Race

'It's so cold, man!' I shuddered as I pulled the zip on my hoodie right up to the neck to shield myself from the cold. Wrapping my arms around my torso to create an added layer I asked, 'do we really have to train in this weather?'

'Yes, we need to. We need to be prepared and ready for the big race!'

Mark and I had been training for the big race that was scheduled for February, two months away. Our daily routine included a punishing six-mile run each morning before most people were even awake. Usually it was okay but this morning the temperature had plummeted to sub-zero and every cell in my body was protesting; but Mark was psyched and rearing to go.

Off we went and if truth be told, after the first mile, the cold was forgotten and slowly I began to enjoy the run. Before we knew it the six miles were completed and we were back home getting ready for the day.

'See how quickly that went?' Mark asked. 'The start is always the hardest part.'

I did not respond because I knew what was coming next: 'I can't wait to whip your ass in this race!'

I laughed out loud, 'must we do this everyday? You only started running a few weeks ago mate; I was born running. I have greater stamina, speed and perseverance, so I think you know how this will turn out. End of!'

We argued back and forth for a few more minutes then went our different ways to our jobs.

§

Finally February came. We eagerly got up and dressed, ready for the day ahead. I chose long jogging bottoms while Mark opted for shorts. We quizzically assessed each other's outfits but neither spoke a word, trying to be polite.

We decided to car-share and at 9am we were on our way to the stadium. We arrived early at 9:30am, just in time to register.

'Good luck Mark. I'll see you at the finish line, mate,' I said as I gently patted his shoulder.

'Thanks Martin Luther King, the dream is still alive!' he chuckled.

We made our way through the crowd that had already gathered to register. There were five registration desks labelled:

- Desk 1 : 100m SPRINTS
- Desk 2 : 400m HURDLES
- Desk 3 : RELAYS
- Desk 4 : STEEPLE CHASE
- Desk 5 : MARATHON

'Hey, can't you read? The sign says "marathon" silly,' Mark shouted, pointing to the sign displayed.

'I can read,' I replied. 'Seems like you can't mate, you're registering for sprints!' I laughed.

We both opened our mouths as realisation hit simultaneously. We had been training for different races.

Final Comments

THIS IS LIFE. Everyone is on their own path, running their own race. Yes, we may train together and run the same trails but we must each must decide our own path.

Most people are always in a competitive frame of mind. They think they need to be better than someone else instead of just being the best they can be. Once you put yourself in a constant competitive mode you are heading for physical, mental and emotional trauma because you will eventually realise that you can never win every time. Life is not about beating someone; it is about recognising who you are and fulfilling your purpose.

The competitive mode also prevents people from helping each other as they believe this will put their competitor ahead. Have you ever worked somewhere and, even though you know you deserve that raise, your boss will never give it to you? Sometimes it is not about you and your hard work; it is about how close you will get to the top.

I was working at a job some time ago and decided to treat myself and purchase a luxurious motorcar. It happened to be the same model as my boss's but bigger, newer and more expensive. Within a week everything I did was criticised and he did everything in his power to discredit me. He was in the competitive mode and did not want to see me in front of him even though I was never competing with him.

How many times have you looked over at the driver in the car next to you with the sole intention of beating them when the light changes, only to realise you are going in different directions? Why is it that when people are in traffic you cannot be in front of them or they will often race you? Bear in mind, you are not going to the same place. Some people are going to work, some people are going home, so why the need to be in front? The finishing line of each is completely different so why is it that some people cannot allow you to go past? They will get in front of you, toot their horn and try to get there first - and then you get to a junction and go your separate ways.

As my son pointed out recently, when we sat trying to analyse the logic behind these actions it is the false feeling of progress that influences people's actions. They like to feel that they are ahead, even though they are going in different directions. You might be going to London from Luton for instance and I might be going to Hemel Hempstead. Even though you are in front of me the fact remains that I am going to get to my destination before you. So, sometimes, why not just chill, enjoy the drive and recognise the fact that everybody is on a different journey and everybody is going to a different place; it would save so much hassle with just that simple acknowledgment.

It is not called the rat race, or the human race without a reason. Every day, without fail, someone somewhere will be competing against you.

CHAPTER 10

The Interview

I rushed excitedly to the office, anxious not to miss this once in a life-time opportunity. After the usual preparations and equipment check we were finally ready.

Finally seated, I came face to face my interviewer who introduced himself as My Rhee Flections and informed me that it would not be a live interview, but would be recorded and edited. I would then be sent the final product, at which point I would be asked to check over each question and answer, and inform them if anything had changed or if I wanted to add any new information.

I agreed and the interview started.

Interviewer: 'Good afternoon Mrs Moulton.'

Mary: 'Good afternoon Mr Flections.'

Interviewer: 'Mary, what three words would your friends used to describe you and why?'

Mary: (a moment's pause) 'Reliable, caring and (another pause) kind - I am reliable because I am always there for others

when they need me; all my friends know
that. Caring because I always check
to make sure they are ok. And kind
because I share what little I have.'

Interviewer: 'Thanks Mary. From the time you
were born until now, how many
lives have you improved?'

Mary: 'I am not sure. What do you
mean by improve?'

Interviewer: 'Made better. How many people, family
excluded by the way, are now in a better
position because they have met you?'

Mary: 'Hmmmm. I do not know. Sorry.'

Interviewer: 'Have you fulfilled all your dreams?'

Mary: 'No, not yet'.

Interviewer: 'Why not?'

Mary: Well I have many dreams but I have a
family and a mortgage so it is not so easy. I
cannot just get up and go chasing after my
dreams. I will start once my kids are grown.'

Interviewer: 'How long?'

Mary: 'In the next five years I think. Yes
definitely in the next five years.'

Interviewer: '................'

Mary: ... 'what?'

Interviewer: 'Nothing. Just thinking how sure you were that you will still be here in five years. Never mind. Mary, how would you want to be remembered when you are gone?'

Mary: 'I do not know but I hope people would remember me as being kind and helpful.'

Interviewer: 'How old are you?'

Mary: 'What?'

Interviewer: 'How old are you?'

Mary: 'Erm - forty-five.'

Interviewer: 'How do you know?'

Mary: 'Well, my birth certificate, driver's licence and my parents told me.'

Interviewer: 'Do you believe them?'

Mary: 'Yes.' (I laugh).

Interviewer: 'What if they all lied? A kind of conspiracy designed to trick you. Do you know the saying; you are as old as you feel? Mary, if you never knew your age, how old would you be and why?'

Mary: 'I guess maybe twenty-five. Why? Because I still feel that young.'

Interviewer: 'If you woke up tomorrow living your life at the age you feel would that affect the decisions you make, and how?'

Mary: 'Wow! I would definitely take more risks and work harder. I guess I would, well, live a little more.'

Interviewer: 'So what you are telling me Mary is that your driver's licence, your birth certificate and parents' information is somehow preventing you from living a fuller life?'

Mary: 'I have never thought about it like that before, but I guess you are right.'

Interviewer: 'Mary, what is it that sustains you physically?'

Mary: 'Can you explain what you mean?'

Interviewer: 'What keeps you alive?'

Mary: 'Food and drink I guess?'

Interviewer: 'Would you drink poison?'

Mary: 'No! Of course not. What type of questions are these?'

Interviewer: 'I am sorry Mary. Just remember nothing will be published without your permission. The questions are designed to get to know the true you. Not the one you think you are but the real Mary. Some of your answers may surprise you when you watch the interview itself. Would you like to continue?'

Mary: 'Yes, ok.'

Interviewer: 'Where were we? Ah yes. Mary, when was the last time you checked the ingredients of the food you consume?'

Mary: 'A good while.'

Interviewer: 'Why? What if you are consuming poison? Do you know who made the bread you ate this morning? I assume you had toast?'

Mary: 'Well no, but I guess someone else checked.'

Interviewer: 'Mary, what is in your hand bag today?'

Mary: 'I know where you are going with this. I know what is in my handbag, but I do not know what is in the food that I put in my body.'

Interviewer: 'Not really, I just wanted to know if you had any tissues, my eyes are watery.'

Mary: 'What?'

Interviewer: 'Just kidding.'

Mary: You are not funny.

Interviewer: 'I know. Mary, you are in sales, correct?'

Mary: 'Yes, we sell cars.'

Interviewer: 'Would you be able to sell me a car, and how would you go about it.'

Mary: 'Well I would ask what you wanted, your budget, intended use etcetera then I would identify cars that would suit you, and go through the features and benefits.'

Interviewer: 'Wow! Sounds impressive. Are cars the
               most important thing you've ever sold?'

Mary: 'Yes, I once sold a car for a million plus.'

Interviewer: 'Wow! But I don't believe you.'

Mary: 'Excuse me?'

Interviewer: Mary your cue card that I am reading
               says you have sold something much
               more expensive every day?

Mary: 'What?'

Interviewer: 'Well Mary, every day we sell ourselves
               to others; by the way we act, dress and
               conduct ourselves. You are a far more
               expensive commodity, would you agree?'

Mary: 'Well yes I do (smile) when
               you put it like that.'

Interviewer: 'I do put it like that Mary. (Smile) Mary
               can you please sell yourself to me
               in two minutes? Give me your best
               marketing pitch, starting now ...'

Mary: 'Aaah! My name is Mary Moulton; I live in
               Pembrokeshire; I am 45 years old; I have
               three children who's names are Anthony,
               Alexander and Tendayi; I have been married
               to Barrington Moulton for over ten years.
               Erm. Erm. I love my job. My favourite show

is Friends and my favourite colour is blue because I love the sky and the sea. I would love to fly my own aeroplane one day or own a boat because I love travelling. (Laughs) 'How many minutes?'

Interviewer: 'Fifty-eight seconds.'

Mary: 'What? Oh my God! It is harder than it sounds.'

Interviewer: 'I would think you know more about yourself than a car?'

Mary: 'I do.'

Interviewer: 'Really? What were the benefits of knowing you? Key features or qualities? What was your USP?'

Mary: 'Well next time I will come more prepared.'

Interviewer: 'Thank you Mary. We will sort the video out and get you a copy as soon as possible.'

Mary: 'You are most welcome.'

End of interview.

Final Comments

1.

Does your age hold you back or prevent you from doing things you would like to accomplish? Age is just a number and should never really define you as a person. There are numerous individuals who achieved their goals at what many would consider middle or old age. On the flip side there are also young people who have already accomplished more than others would in a life time. What if these success stories had lived by the number on their birth certificate instead of what they felt inside?

Start working towards your dreams today. Stop and check where you are today then reflect on where you were one year ago. Have you made any positive steps towards accomplishing all your goals? Now fast forward to a year from now and decide what you need to accomplish and start moving. Not tomorrow or next week, NOW! Stop, check and reflect; then go!

Remember if you want to be a millionaire and put just £1 in your savings account, you no longer need a million pounds, now you only need £999,999 to become a millionaire.

2.

My grandmother used to ask me three questions when I was growing up, to help me to see who I am and how others see me. Her questions were:

- Can you give me three words you would use to describe yourself?
- Can you give me three words your family would use to describe you?
- Can you give me three words your friends would use to describe you?

My Gran felt that even though we are different and act differently depending on who were are with, our core personality always shine through. If you are kind hearted you know it, your family may experience it, and your friends should believe it. Regardless of how we act, everyone should be aware of it.

If we answer those three questions honestly, most people find that the three questions give three different words. My Gran felt that at least two of those words should be the same for all three questions at some point in your life; if they are wildly different we should use the first three as our core descriptors, and ensure others see it as well.

How many times have we heard people saying that they are misunderstood or they express shock at how others perceive them? Truth is sometimes who we believe we are; what others see and experience can be a completely different person.

Start living as the person you want to be remembered as today.

3.

Selling yourself is what you do on a daily basis by the way you portray yourself to others. Since it is the most important sell of your life, ensure you know your product well. Know the strengths, benefits, the weakness and flaws so that you know what you are selling.

Remember, when you walk into a room the value you place on your self will be reflected in the way you stand, speak and interact with other people. Do not undervalue yourself.

I can guarantee that you have done many positive things - touched lives, accomplished goals - but do not even remember them. Have you filled a job application in, and after you have sent the form you remembered something you did not include? You must always know more about yourself than anything else.

4

Your health is your most priceless possession. Take care of you. Know the types of food you consume and ensure your body remains fit. Remember it makes no sense if you gain the world but cannot enjoy it.

One of the instructions given in case of an emergency on board a plane is to fit your gas mask first before attempting to help others.

Questions to reflect on:

- Is your age holding you back?
- How will others remember you once you are gone?
- Are you selling yourself at your true market value?
- Do you know your product?
- Are you keeping yourself in the best possible condition?

CHAPTER 11

The Movie

Yesterday I watched the most boring movie of my life. It was highly anticipated and billed to be a huge success. I never like biographies but this one I had to see, I had no choice. I sat waiting for it to start, anxious to get a move on.

The movie finally started with the birth of a young girl on some tropical island and her early years were pretty much uneventful, the usual mundane details:

Forming and breaking friendships.

Falling in and out of love, going to school etcetera.

Nothing that really engaged the audience I thought. It could have been any random person's life. There was nothing that was memorable or worth remembering. I quickly forgot it.

I wanted to press pause at times, just to get a break, but my remote somehow would not work. There were times I missed a beautiful moment in my anxiety to rush the development of the plot, to get to the good stuff. I sometimes wished I could rewind but the controls were too far away and I was too lazy to move. I was also tempted many times to turn off the television but I kept saying there must be more. I kept waiting for the plot to unfold.

The advert had said exciting, life changing, unique, never before seen; so there just had to be more.... and so I continued to watch in eager anticipation. Ten minutes and nothing, twenty minutes and nothing, thirty minutes still nothing.

Waiting, waiting, waiting but it just dragged on and on. It almost became embarrassing. Whoever wrote this script should definitely be sacked.

The lead character grew up, went to college, got married, started a family and started working. She did not really enjoy the job, but kept going and going and going. How dumb! What a waste of time, I thought.

This had to be the most boring movie ever. No competitor anywhere.

After forty-three minutes I finally had enough; it got too much for me. So in anger, frustration and disappointment I slowly moved away from my mirror.

§

Today I finally started the sequel and so far it is much better. I have started chasing my dreams.

Watch this space! Part two promises to be much, much more exciting!

<u>*Final Comments*</u>

Stop for five minutes somewhere quiet. No, STOP!!

Seek out somewhere quiet and use the moment to reflect. What have you done with your life so far? If you watched your life like you watched movies, how exciting would it be?

Would it be a blockbuster or a complete and utter flop? It is never too late to start. Some movies start out with a bang but the sequels are not as good as the first or they are complete and utter failures. *The Matrix* was one example; many think the sequel did not live up to expectations. This is similar to people who did everything in their youth but waste the later years of their lives.

Then there are those who got off to a slow start, then find themselves and became a huge success. Just like *Star Wars*; the first one was good but when *The Empire Strikes Back* was made it made the *Star Wars* series famous.

The best movies however are the ones that retain smash-hit status throughout the sequels. Just like the *Harry Potter* series where all the movies were very good. This is how we should aim to live life: every day should be a success worthy of a box office hit!

CHAPTER 12

The Traffic Lights

I was driving back from Aylesbury sometime in September 2015 and took the scenic route to get back home to Luton.

I was rocking to some classic Gregory Isaacs, one of my many reggae icons, when I came to a very narrow bridge and a red traffic light, so I slowly came to a stop.

I was at the front of the queue and very soon other vehicles started lining up behind me. Before I knew it, I had a long queue patiently waiting at my rear.

After about five minutes I started getting impatient. The traffic coming in the opposite direction had ceased three minutes ago. Why was the light still red? Was it broken?

I waited for another three minutes but still the light was on red. At that point I rationalised the risk of trying to go through the red light even though I could not see over the bridge and around the corner.

I slowly eased off the brake and started inching forward, cautiously.

Then, as soon as I got closer, the red light immediately changed to green allowing me to go through.

I related the incident to a friend later that day and he explained what happened.

Apparently the stoplights were operated using motion sensors. I had stopped my car too far back and so the light remained on red because the sensors did not pick up that a car was there. The lights therefore remained on red. As soon as I started moving closer they sensed the vehicle and changed to green, allowing me to go through. If I had not moved closer, I would still be waiting at that red light.

Final Comments

As I reflected on my experience I could see some similarities in how we approach things sometimes.

In life, when problems arise, we tend to stop in our tracks waiting for the problem to go away or for someone else to solve it for us. At times we hide away or look in another direction, refusing to acknowledge we have a problem.

We need to realise that if we cautiously approach the problem then a solution usually presents itself. Think back on your life about some of the problems you have experienced, the problems you thought were too big and you would never get through. Where are they now? Have they not shrunk in size or disappeared altogether?

The fact that you are still here and reading this means those problems were solved, are being solved or will soon be solved. There are very few, if any, problems in this world that have no solution (mathematicians may disagree!). Think about it for a while.

There is always a solution, even if you do not agree with it.

CHALLENGE

Face your problems; do not hide from them. Inch forward slowly and cautiously. A solution will present itself.

CHAPTER 13

The Pawn

Let me teach you a new game today I pleaded with my ten-year-old son.

'But Mom I would prefer to play Connect 4, 'he grumpily replied.

'Yes I know hon but that game is more for six-year-olds. How about a game that most adults can't even play? You'll be one of the smartest boys in your school,' I said cheekily, using my A level psychology. 'Imagine being able to play a game that most of your mates can't? You might even get one over on your teacher as well.'

'Mom, please!' he replied indignantly. 'First of all board games are so 1950's.' I winced. 'Everyone I know is into playing with their X Box 360, or video games. No one plays board games anymore,' he replied. Clearly he had strong arguments.

But when did mothers give up after just two tries? Never.

Time to use my ace card otherwise I was certain to lose face: the authority ace. 'Look here, my lovely son, I am your mother and I am going to teach you this game today, so let it go. The longer our arguments drag on the less time you'll have left to do whatever else you might actually like to do.'

With the usual subtle roll of the eyes and the drooping shoulders he reluctantly agreed. I would take any victory I could. 'Learn this and then we can go to McDonalds,' I added as a deal-sweetener. I was rewarded by a thinly disguised fake smile.

'Ok ok!' he replied. 'Let's get on with it.'

Not easily deterred I plodded on. 'Firstly, these are all the pieces and these are the way they move.' It took ten minutes of telling, showing, questioning and demonstrating before my son understood all the moves, the names of each piece, their positions and their value. He knew the king should be protected at all costs, the queen was the most versatile, the knight was the only piece to jump over the heads of other pieces down to the lowest chess piece, the lowly pawn which could only move one place at a time and take another piece diagonally.

Finally sorted, we started our first game of chess. I was thrilled to have taught Stephan this game and I smiled to myself. There was no strategy for our first game; it was just about playing a friendly game and getting used to each piece. We moved at each turn and after a while it came down to just swapping pieces. He took my knight and in the next two moves I had his bishop. I kept moving forward with all my pieces. After an hour the board pieces were very scanty but Stephan had managed to protect his king with just a bishop, four pawns, a knight and a rook.

On my side I had my king, a bishop, two pawns a knight and a rook.

My son looked at the time and asked for a break. Mercifully I complied. His face opened into a huge grin. He looked at the board and said 'Looks like I win, Mom!'

'How do you figure that?'

'Look at the value of the pieces I have left compared to yours,' he stated with confidence, directing his gaze to the board. 'I have two more pawns than you.'

Following his gaze I looked on the board. 'That's true,' I replied. 'You do have two more pawns than me. But sweetie look at my two pawns … they are standing on your back line!'

Final Comments

I suspect those who do not know chess will be left slightly puzzled here. Allow me to add a bit of clarity. If in a chess game you can successfully manoeuvre your pawn to the backline of your opponent's game then you are allowed to change that pawn into any piece you like except a king. So your pawn can become another queen.

Sometimes you may not hold the same qualification, position, or know the right people; you may be seen as a mere pawn in the game of chess. Others around you may have the freedom to move in many different directions and some may even jump over the heads of others while trying to get to where they want to be.

Your progress may be slow and seem unimportant, but, if you can, just focus and be patient when your path is blocked and wait until the way is clear. Just keep moving one step at a time.

Be patient with yourself and others and keep focussed on your goal. Eventually you will get there. Some may still see you as a pawn without even realising where you are standing.

So although Stephan had more pawns, mine were better placed strategically.

In life sometimes we may look like mere pawns to others and they may treat us as such.

But never be doubtful about the potential that exists within you. As you go through your daily life, just keep on moving.

If you are working a job without any potential for growth, start studying, start saving, start doing something so when the day comes for your detractors to shout that you are just a pawn, you are prepared to say 'yes, I might look that way but just look where I'm standing. I am standing in a position ready to shake off my pawn status and walk into my own'.

CHAPTER 14

My Dream Job

'Aaaaah! Yessssssss!' I screamed at the top of my lungs.

My friends all rushed out breathlessly to check if I was okay.

'I got it! I got it!' I yelled with glee. 'I got my dream job.' I could not be more excited. This had to be the happiest moment of my life. Jumping up and down on the sofa I am sure they thought I had completely lost my mind.

'What job?' asked Sofia.

'I'm going to get my movie made. I wrote the entire script, well almost. Mom and Dad got me started and helped a bit at the beginning, paying bills, being my taxi amongst other things but for the most part I wrote everything else.'

At nineteen I had finished writing my very own movie. 'Success! Success!' I had the widest grin ever.

'Well then, what is the movie about?' Brad the second of my nosey drinking buddies enquired.

'It's not a long movie but I think it's great. It's about a girl born into a middle-class family and for the first ten years there was nothing extraordinary about it. At eleven she began going off the rails and breaking all the rules. Despite many warnings and repeated requests from parents, friends, teachers and family she kept on breaking the rules. She started drinking and pretty soon got into drugs.

She finally cleaned up her life at eighteen but became withdrawn and a recluse. She shared all her desires and dreams with all her best friends and finally she enrolled in college, tried to get back on track and make her family proud. But her past eventually came back to haunt her.

Then one night it all changed. It changed with an ear shattering scream "Aaaaah! Yessssssss!" as her room mates, Brad and Sofia rushed out to see what was the matter. They stopped in shock at the grim sight of their roommate lying on the floor, dead from cocaine overdose.'

The movie of her life was over.'

Final Comments

How will the movie of your life sound? Best seller or box office flop?

Decide now!

CHAPTER 15

What if There Was No Pharaoh?

I was sharing with my Mom recently, telling her about all the obstacles in my life. She reminded me of a story I had heard over twenty years ago.

The story was about a king.

One morning a woman went to the king and said 'Oh king I can't take it any more. I have too many problems and I can't deal with them. I must have the hardest life by far in your entire kingdom I'm sure.'

The king listened and promised he would give it some deep thought and find a remedy for her problems soon, and away she went.

Within the next hour there was another knock at the king's door and in walked a young man. 'Sire, I am heavily burdened,' he said. 'My wife is always nagging, the children are so rude and my neighbour loves to quarrel. So many problems that I'm certain I'm the one who has the greatest problems in your entire kingdom.'

The king once again listened. 'Go back to your home,' he replied. 'I will consider all these problems and find you a solution soon.'

It was not long before another person came to the king and said the same thing. By the end of the day the king had fifty people complaining about their many problems, each believing that their problems were the worst by far.

So the king thought long and hard over the next two days. Then he sent for everyone who had complained about their problems to him.

When they had all gathered he said, 'this is my solution. Everyone go to your respective homes and pack every one of your problems into one bag, lock it tightly and return tomorrow with all your problems securely fastened.'

Off they went to their homes. The first lady went home and packed her son who was twenty and had never worked a day in his life, she put in her leaky roof, her husband's drinking habits and her low wages. She packed up it all in one bag and locked it tightly.

Bright and early the next morning she headed to the king's castle. On her way she could see many others with similar bundles. When they arrived at the castle the king instructed everyone to stand in a straight line at the end of a vast field. At the other end he strung a long rope with each end tied to a great big oak tree.

The king then instructed everyone to run down to the rope and tie their bags of problems onto it, then come up to the starting line. Everyone rushed to tie up their bags before returning to the start.

The king then said, 'I want you to stand here for five minutes and look at the line of problems at the far end of this field. When I say "go," I want you to run as fast as possible and grab the lightest bag of problems you see.' Everyone started staring at the line, trying to decide whose problems they would rather have.

The rich man who lived in the mansion started looking at the problems of the young man who lived in a one room flat; he could not understand how the young man's bag could be so big. After all, he did not pay as much taxes, pay for servants or work as much as the rich man did. Surely he could not have as many problems? 'He has only one room; I have many more rooms to deal with, therefore his bag cannot be that big; my bag has to be the bigger.'

The homeless woman started looking at the woman living in the three-bedroom house in a nice neighbourhood with her husband and three lovely children. She was puzzled as to the size of the other woman's bag; it was so heavy it almost touched the ground. The other woman must be lying she concluded. 'I do not have a home, a loving husband or children and those were the biggest problems anyone could encounter in life.'

The rich man never realised that the young man living in that one room had just days to live. The homeless woman did not realise that other lady was being beaten each night nor the extent of her debts and that she wished she could leave that pretty house and sleep under the stars just as she had done before both parents died.

In time each person's gaze drifted slowly back to their own bag of problems. They now realised how small their own bag was. When the king felt enough time had elapsed. He shouted, 'ready, set go!' and everyone ran as fast as they could, grabbed their own bag of problems and headed straight back home knowing that everybody had their own problems, some more than they realised.

(story adapted)

Final Comments

Sometimes we may have so many problems that it weighs us down and we feel as if we cannot make it.

Then we speak to someone else and the realisation hits us: every single person has their own problems that they are carrying. The only difference is that we each carry them differently.

There is no one without a problem. The problems might be different though; for some people it is immigration; some have financial problems; some are having problems with their family or relationships; or some may just have a leaking roof. Everybody has some kind of problem in their life.

It is important for us to realise that problems are masked opportunities. Some people remain in the same job for years because they are comfortable and have no real problems to deal with. If their boss had created a bit of problem for them then they would have started looking for something better, or working harder to get where they wanted to be. When people adopt the lifestyle of "if it ain't broke don't fix it" they settle into complacency and never fulfil their true potential. Usain Bolt may have never achieved the world record without competitors in his races; he would not have needed to run so fast.

From a religious perspective I have asked myself on numerous occasions, 'when those Israelites came to the Red Sea, what if God had not hardened Pharaoh's heart?' God intervened and created a problem for the fleeing Israelites. Had there not been that problem when they came to the Red Sea those Israelites would probably have just camped right there or taken an alternative route and perished.

Be grateful for the people or things in your life that causes you a bit of angst sometimes. It is sometimes the push you need to get started towards finding your happiness, fulfilment or purpose.

CHAPTER 16

Which Coffee Are You?

There have been many metaphors adopted to explain mankind, their emotions, idiosyncrasies, relationships and the way they act or respond in given situations. With the complexity of mankind, almost all metaphors have very glaring inconsistencies or limitations.

By far the best representation I have found to explain mankind is coffee. Sounds too simple? Maybe.

On a recent shopping trip my Mom and eldest son attempted to describe a family friend and just could not find the right words. My Mom started describing the object of their conversation by saying the person can never get straight to the point in any conversation. Every time they spoke she had to wait before he would get to the actual conversation.

My son immediately piped up, 'just like a cappuccino, right Mom?' Momentarily we all paused as we searched to find the similarity and a visual of a cappuccino. After a few seconds of reflective silence we all concluded with a resounding, 'yes, just like a cappuccino.'

We all laughed at the description. Mom then asked me what type of coffee would I be?

I thought for a moment then asked, 'I don't know. How many types of coffee can there be?'

It sounded simple enough but as soon as I got home I went to the internet to find out how many different types of coffee there are. Apparently there exists quite a wide variety of shades, complexity and types of coffee. The word "coffee" itself comes from the Arabic word قوهق *qahwah*.

According to the Huffington Post, February 10, 2014, there are about thirty-eight different types of coffee drinks or derivatives, which is quite remarkable, as they all come from the coffee bean.

I can almost guarantee there is one that matches your personality. Here is a summary of the main types of coffees, which one are you?

Café au Lait

This is the pampered coffee, very posh indeed. Underneath the surface these types are the same as every one of us, but they possess the added extras and so parade around as if they are more privileged than everyone else. While others drive the normal people carriers or family car they are driving the top end motor vehicles that cost as much as a house. They dine on pâté while the rest of the world eats crushed liver.

ESPRESSO

Looks small but is packed full of punch. Do not let the size fool you, it says exactly what it does; it delivers. This slightly contradicts the old adage that size matters but clearly adds credence to the fact that good things come in small packages. If you are an espresso then you should be taken in small doses and not messed around; as they can give as well as they can take.

Espresso reminds me of my mother. Strong and to the point and will keep you awake all night.

RISTRETTO.

Not very popular and most people might not even know this type of coffee. Ristretto types are blunt, no diplomacy, and straight to the point. If you cannot stand an espresso then completely stay clear of these people. They are espresso plus!

LONG BLACK

These are twice what an espresso brings. This type are not messed with, or messed around. Crossing their path is asking for trouble. Not double the strength but definitely double the size. These are the really abrasive people and they have the muscle to prove it.

Mocha

These are the real deal but with added sweetness to take the edge off. For people who fall into the mocha category they are usually confident with who they are. They do not walk around flexing muscles and will carry an old lady's shopping but they can switch when they need to.

I have met a few mochas in my time. They are mixed; not pure coffee and not pure hot chocolate. They sit on the fence.

Irish coffee

These are the wild ones. If you are throwing a party then these are the people you want there. They bring the life to the party. They are not afraid to break the rules.

Café Machiatto

Literally translated it means "stained coffee" I will leave the subject there.

Frappé

It is said that this coffee was accidentally invented and the story goes on to say it is preferred by youths. Frappé is the hip and trendy type. They do not plan; they just live day to day.

TURKISH COFFEE

These are unfiltered. They are not as polished as the café au lait's of this world, but will settle into any food company quite nicely. You may never see their unpolished personalities unless you decide to shake the cup then you will know very quickly how unpolished they are. Handle with caution, slow and steady does it. This type is a bit rough. They will adapt to their surroundings but if tested you will soon realise they are not what they seem.

CAPPUCCINO

These are a dangerous type. They don't blow up easily. When they get angry, all the heat is kept inside. They are always over the top in whatever they do. They are quite popular but everyone knows not to cross them and it drives you crazy waiting for them to cool down.

They usually ramble on a bit before they get down to business, covered in froth because of the processes they go through. Once you drink a cappuccino you get the coffee but the foam is left on your lip as a reminder and stays there until you wipe it off.

FLAT WHITE

This type are not about sucking up. Similar to the cappuccinos but contain much less froth. A good flat white is all about packing as much taste as possible into a small package. Straight to the point.

Mazagran.

These are cold. They get the job done because they have what it takes but are emotionless. This type are not ruled by their emotions. They just do what is required. Good workers, especially where one is not required to show any type of emotion.

Decaffeinated

These are the pretenders. They do not actually belong in your group because they have no substance. They wear masks and appear to blend in but actually do not contribute anything to the success and growth of anything. They have zero effect on the situation.

§

Coffee is definitely like people. Such a wide range and but each comes in different sizes, has different strengths and varying effects.

I have concluded that I am a black coffee. Ground, not instant! There is a bit of hard work in getting me to a certain level but worth every ounce of effort. If I get into hot water, I change the water. I make my presence known.

CHAPTER 17

House for Rent

HOUSE FOR RENT.

PLEASE APPLY WITHIN.

REQUIREMENTS: UNDERSTANDING, PATIENT AND KIND. MUST BE ABLE TO SHARE FACILITIES. LONG TERM TENANCY PREFERRED BUT SHORT TERM CAN BE CONSIDERED.

It was clearly a multiple occupancy house. I had just broken up with my third girlfriend in as many months and was anxious for a quick escape to a new place. I circled the ad. and decided to ring on my break.

§

'Hello, I am ringing about the room advertised.'

'Oh yes, it's still available. Can you stop by to have a look?' she asked.

'I can after work today. Say about 5pm?'

'Yes that's fine. I'm Sophia, what's your name?'

'Peter,' I replied.

'Ok Peter, see you at five.'

§

Ding-dong went the old doorbell, quickly answered by a lady who appeared to be in her early thirties. Very pretty but clearly had a rough life. Still, not bad I thought.

'Hi, I'm Sophia.'

'Peter.' I responded offering my hand.

'Come in. I'll give you a quick tour,' she smiled and my heart fluttered for some unknown reason. I followed her inside.

Omar lived in the room at the back on the ground floor. He was clearly being well cared for because he had the second biggest room in the house. From all indications it seemed he was the manager for the entire house.

Mark, Peter and JT were also living on the same floor but they just visited from time to time as they were all cramped in one room together. I asked them why they had to share a room and they explained they were never there at the same time. They were all different personalities, shapes and attitudes but they shared one thing: they all lived in fear of Omar. His room overshadowed theirs and it was clear Sophia valued his input more than any other.

On the first floor it looked like an office building. There was a lady shouting loudly as if she owned the entire place. Sophia timidly and quietly whispered, 'that is Mrs Johnson. She owns the company I work for but she's so mean. I never challenge her, I don't like confrontations so I just leave her be.'

'But since you own the building, why don't you give her notice?' I enquired. 'She seems so mean.'

'I don't know,' she replied nervously twisting her hands. 'Maybe one day but let's go quickly. I hate to upset her.'

We climbed to the second floor. 'This is the best floor,' she smiled. 'I live on this floor.'

I expected her room to be the biggest and most elaborate since she was in charge of the entire building but she was squeezed into the tiniest room I have ever seen. Even the room shared by Mark, Peter and JT was bigger. There was barely room to move and it was filled to the brim.

'Is this the top floor?' I asked.

'No, the penthouse is above.'

'Well, who lives there?' I asked.

'My parents and family.'

'Should we go up and meet them?'

'Of course not. They never liked to be disturbed. Mom is busy with my sisters. They are absolutely beautiful; here's a picture.'

The picture shows two beautiful blonde girls with sparkling blue eyes. She answered the question before I asked.

'Yes I know. They look nothing like me. I'm not so pretty. Many think my mother cheated and I was the result. That's why I live out of the way; they never visit.'

'But why not ask them to leave? It is your house right?'

'Yes but it's comforting knowing they are there.'

'Where would I live?' I enquired.

She opened an empty room near to her cubicle. 'Here,' she said. 'No one has ever lived here before.'

It was a beautiful place and it was hard to understand why she had never rented this space before.

I agreed to move in but in my heart I knew I would need to help her organise this place and evict some people if needs be.

'How much is the rent?' I asked.

Her answer came as the biggest shock of all. 'It's free!' she replied.

'Does everyone live free?'

'Yes they do,' she replied lowering her gaze to the floor.

Final Comments

Living free is a concept many of us will not be familiar with unless we are living with family or exceptional friends. Everything has a cost, be it monetary, service related, emotional or mental; a price must be paid. So if you own a property and everyone is living rent-free, it means you are the one making all the required payments.

The question here is how many people are living rent free in your life?

How many people are living in your head rent free?

Who occupies most of your thought on a daily basis? Are they relevant or important to your life? Still thinking about that ex that did you wrong, or your boss who makes your life miserable?

It is important that you ensue when you think of people you do not elevate them to a position higher than they belong. Some people should be forgotten as quickly as you meet them or given limited time and space in your life. Never be afraid to evict people who have stopped contributing to your existence or are making a nuisance of themselves.

There are times when, despite physically removing people from our lives, or even if they have removed themselves, we continue to hold onto the memories. They become such a part of us that we might even start to judge others based on the memories we hold. By letting them occupy a large space in your mind you may sometimes end up blocking others that may want to come into your life and make a positive contribution.

Start the eviction process today!

CHAPTER 18

Did the Right Sperm Win?

What are the odds of being struck by lightning?

What are the odds of winning the lottery?

What are the odds of you living until one hundred?

Many millions to one; the likelihood of any one of the above happening to you is very remote. But what are the greatest odds you will ever face in your life?

The greatest odds you will ever face is being conceived.

Imagine over one hundred million sperms released with the sole object of finding an egg to create YOU. Each sperm will have completely different genetic material and can end up creating completely different individuals. But in the end only one sperm can win, and the one that won this race is the one that created you.

Was it an accident? Why did this particular sperm win? Why were you created?

I do not believe there are accidents in the creation of life. Each individual has a specific purpose to fit somewhere in the jigsaw called life.

But sadly many of us die without fulfilling this purpose

and in the end the brutal question must be asked: "Did the Right Sperm Win?"

If you are not working to the best of your ability or trying to accomplish all that you can then you are not showing the world that the right sperm won. If another sperm won, would they have made a greater contribution to this world?

The challenge is yours today. Show the world that the right sperm won the race.

CHAPTER 19

I Will Pray For You

'Oh My God! Oh My God! Don't jump. Please don't jump.'

'Listen to me. It's not worth it; whatever it is, it's not worth it. Talk to me, don't cry, and let's just talk... Someone help us!'

In desperation I looked around. It had been raining heavily and at 9 pm most people were either inside wrapped up warmly or in the pub waiting out the rain. It was by chance I took the wrong turn on my way home after a late night at the office. I just happened to glance up, to see if there was a slight change in the clouds.

At first I did not recognise what I was seeing; squinting my eyes so I could block the rain drops from blinding me I saw the young man on the ledge of the third floor balcony.

Without hesitation or thought I jumped out of my car and ran up three flights of stairs.

Within minutes I was out in the rain talking to this stranger. He appeared to be a young man no older than twenty. He stood there at the edge of the building; head bowed, rain pelting down.

'Oh My God! Oh My God! Don't jump. Please don't jump.'

'Listen to me. It's not worth it; whatever it is, it's not worth it. Talk to me, don't cry, and let's just talk... Someone help us!'

'Nothing ever goes right for me,' he muttered. I felt there was a slight chance to save him when he responded. I had read somewhere that communication is the first step in solving any problems; he was opening up.

'Tell me what's wrong.'

'My parents hate me because I am gay. I failed all my exams. Today my boss fired me and with no income it is only a matter of time before I'm evicted. Who would miss me?'

'I would young man.'

We turned in unison to see a middle-aged Hispanic woman silhouetted in the doorway to the rooftop.

'Sorry? Who are you?' The boy asked.

She slowly walked forward and her face became clear to us. I looked towards the guy on the ledge for any hint of recognition in his expression.

'Hello Mrs Mint,' he said.

'Son, nothing, nothing, is worth taking your life for. God loves you. These storms you are going through will pass. This is just a test.'

The young man started sobbing but he did take a step back from the ledge. 'Mrs Mint I feel so alone and... depressed.'

'I will pray for you,' Mrs Mint replied.

The young man on the ledge did not see the resemblance to the boy he loved. The boy who had broken his heart because his family did not approve of him and hated him.

The three of us stood on the balcony each waiting, each thinking. Mrs Mint prayed silently as the distant sirens drew closer: 'Lord cast down my enemies'.

Final Comments

Communication is the key. We must always ensure we understand what the other person means when they use certain words. One word or phrase can convey many meanings depending on the intonation of the voice, how it is written or even the accompanying body language.

Have you ever stopped to ask some when they tell you, 'I am going to pray for you,' exactly what they mean? What are they praying for?

The Bible has many inspiring words that can lift the spirit and as a Christian I do believe committed Christians can intercede on one's behalf. But has anyone ever read for example, all the psalms, all 150 of them?

What if someone prays and reads Psalm 109 for you? How pleased would you be?

CHAPTER 20

The Jigsaw

Sunday afternoon is family time and today it was Ethan's turn to choose the game. We all took turns each Sunday. We waited for the youngest member of the family to choose, although we all knew what his choice would be. The same game he chose every week when he was asked to make the decision.

'Jigsaw!' he yelled, and then we all pretended it was the most exciting game ever and we could hardly wait to play. At five years old it is one of the simplest games and one that he thinks he plays well.

We get all five hundred of the pieces of the jigsaw on the table and the entire family of Mom, Jonathan, Matthew and me start the sorting.

As Ethan is just starting to recognising colours I ask him to group the pieces according to similar colours to make an easier start. Everyone knows that there is a higher probability that similar colours will be close to each other.

After sorting the colours we start to assemble the puzzle and having had over twenty practice runs from previous Sundays we soon start putting a section of the picture together.

Ethan seeing my attempt to complete a picture of a red rose attempts to put another red piece in an available slot. The piece does actually fit nicely into the available space but when you take a quick overview it is clear that it just does not belong there.

'Ethan.' Mom tried to explain, 'it doesn't go there sweetie.'

'But it's red and it's the right shape,' he retorted, pouting petulantly and refusing to move the piece he had skilfully manoeuvred into place.

'Mom!' I cried for assistance. After numerous attempts to explain to Ethan, Mom suggested we leave the piece for now and continue with the puzzle. In time, she explained, another space will open and Ethan will realise exactly where that piece belongs. So we continued putting pieces of the puzzle together and we could see the puzzle slowly starting to look like the picture of the garden on the box. After about an hour Jonathan shouted, 'Ethan stop it!' We looked over to see Ethan busily squeezing another piece that clearly did not fit; neither in shape nor colour into an available space.

'No Ethan,' I cried, taking the piece away. 'Now look! You've bent the edges of this piece and look, you've also bent the edges of the other pieces where you were squeezing this one in.'

Ethan became upset and left to sit on his own. Clearly the fun had slowly dissipated and the game had now become a chore. After another hour we finally completed the puzzle; eventually Ethan even realised his mistake and returned to move the first piece to its rightful position.

'Monopoly next week, it's my turn to choose,' Jonathan shouted.

'I'm sure this was meant to be fun but I think it's time for something new, Mom,' I said as I started breaking the jigsaw apart and packing the pieces away.

Final Comments

"LIFE IS LIKE A JIGSAW PUZZLE, THERE ARE NO EXTRA PIECES IN THE BOX.
TRY AND FIND EXACTLY WHERE YOU BELONG."

VINETTE HOFFMAN-JACKSON

Sometimes in life we try to fit into places we do not belong. We figure that we are the right shape, we look the same, have the same qualifications, background, similar culture so we must belong. But if we just take a step backward or try to see the bigger picture we soon realise that we do not belong where we think we do. It may be your job, with your partner, your geographical location or even with your current friends. Everything seems right to others looking in but you do not feel comfortable in that space. Going to work or home has become a chore and you get easily irritated and start wishing your life away. The simple fact is you may not belong there and it is time to start moving.

Like Ethan sometimes we try to force ourselves into spaces where we clearly do not belong because we have no patience to wait; or the energy, motivation or finances to continue searching for our rightful place. You may have got the job through who you know and so end up rubbing everyone the wrong way. It may be a situation where you are the boss and no one really likes you. They fear you instead of respect you, but you want to exert your power so you remain in the job anyway.

The result is we not only cause damage to others but end up damaging ourselves in the process. We squeeze into that promotion given because we know the right people; get married because everyone expects it. We end up being miserable and making others around us miserable too. When we are squeezed somewhere we do not belong we become restless, short tempered and constantly moan about things. The solution is to start moving in an effort to find your true place. Find out what your skills are, what you enjoy and start planning your life.

The two worst things about remaining where you do not belong is that you are not only occupying someone else's place and preventing them from fulfilling their purpose; but your place has been left unoccupied and your purpose remains unfulfilled.

Find where you belong!

CHAPTER 21

Labels

'Blaaaargh! Blaaaaaaarrrrgghh!'

'It's getting worst,' I snickered, 'by the time she's finished, her spleen will be in that toilet bowl!'

'Blaaaargh! Blaaaaaaarrrrgghh!' the retching sounds emanated from the bathroom.

'Stick two fingers down your throat,' Melody advised.

'Don't encourage her,' I begged.

I did not have the nerve to tell her that whatever she had eaten had long since been absorbed into her cells; in fact she was now whatever she had eaten. The thought made me chuckle out loud.

'Blaaaargh! Blaaaaaaarrrrgghh! Blaaaargh! Blaaaaaaarrrrgghh!'

I wonder how long it would continue before she realised her efforts were futile.

Not as long as I imagined. She slowly emerged from the toilet with a towel wrapped around her mouth as if she half expected to vomit any time soon. I smiled, 'feeling better Susie?' I enquired with as much sincerity as I could decently fake.

'What do you think?' she shot back, 'I bet you're just gloating at this aren't you? Why don't you say I told you so? I know you want to say it.'

For years I have begged Susie to reduce her consumption of fast food and processed meals with no success, but where I failed the BBC succeeded; I will take my victories wherever I can get them.

'I will never ever eat another processed meal! HORSE MEAT!' she screamed, 'I can't believe they would let me eat HORSE MEAT!'

I smiled into a delicately placed cushion. 'Victory!' I whispered.

Final Comments

The Horsemeat scandal of 2013 certainly reverberated around the globe with various memes, jokes and magazine articles. It was a shock to many, and new rules, tests and regulations were immediately implemented.

The lesson learnt; we cannot always trust labels. Sometimes it is not what it says on the box.

How many of us judge people by the way they look, how they speak, their jobs, education, where they live or what they wear? We tend to group people according to our limited experiences and knowledge. Sometimes we even believe other people's assessment of others without stopping to check for ourselves if the label being presented is accurate.

We should always be careful about putting labels on people because we might be putting the wrong labels; we do not truly know what is inside.

Allow people to write their own labels. Sometimes who a person was ten years ago is completely different from whom they are now but the same old label has not been changed. This can lead us into all sorts of problems. I have known high school sweethearts who went their separate ways then by chance happened to meet twenty years later. Each remembered the person they knew and made an attempt at a relationship, only to realise it was a horrible mistake. Failing to check if the label is correct or up to date can be quite painful.

We also need to realise that as in some countries the labels may not contain enough information, and so we may not trust the product inside. People sometimes write their own labels in order to sway your decisions which we may later regret. On the flip side some people in writing their own labels downplay their full value and lose out.

Being careful, however, does not mean being stupid; I would not recommend eating a *Fruit and Nut* chocolate bar if you have a severe nut allergy.

Err on the side of caution advises the old adage.

CHAPTER 22

The Phoenix Point

I attended my son's prize-giving some years back and the keynote speaker started his address with a lovely story I wanted to share. He told the story of a coach at half time trying to rally his team to victory.

§

The coach gathered his football team together for a half time pep talk after being down four goals to nil.

'Boys,' he rallied, 'we are down and it looks very dark and gloomy. It may even look like there's no way out of this one. Many teams would give up at this point but remember when everything seems lost and you are at the bottom, then the only way to go is up! So come on lads shake off the dust and the ashes and let us rise up like a pheasant from those ashes and soar.'

'C-c- coach,' the new boy interrupted, 'do you mean phoenix?'

'What?' the coach glared at young Thompson.

'The bird, it's called a phoenix, sir. That's the name of the bird that rises from the ashes!'

The coached looked at the young man as if he would strangle him right there in the dressing room but was deterred only by the number of witnesses in the room.

'Thompson!' the coach thundered, 'don't bother me with trivialities. I don't care what the bird was. I just know it was one of those birds that starts with an "F".'

They won the game six-four.

Long live the phea... phoenix!

Final Comments

Let us face it, everyone has those days, months or even years when nothing seems to go right. Evictions, repossessions, bankruptcy, broken relationships, job dissatisfaction, natural disasters, sickness etcetera and the list goes on. Many people give up at these low points. They may drift into depression, give up, or decide life is no longer worth living.

They fail to realise that nature's favourite shape is a circle and if you find yourself at the bottom of that wheel it will only be a matter of time before you are back at the top; provided you keep that wheel turning. The secret is to make sure you have enough in you to ride out the next turn of the wheel. No one stay on top indefinitely. If it is not one thing, it will be something else. Understand that nobody has a perfect life.

It is at these low points that some people realise when you are at the bottom then the only way is up. For some people these are the moments when they stop their moaning and dwelling in self-pity and start that wheel spinning again. This is what I like to call their "phoenix point". This is when they rise from the ashes, shake off the dust, broken dreams, broken promises and misfortunes and decide to start working to make it back to the top.

Your phoenix point may come in many forms; you just need to recognise it. For some people it might be the realisation that your children are totally dependent on you and you cannot let them down. For others it may just be the motivation to prove all your doubters and haters wrong; it may be a religious revelation or it may just be a kind word, a simple observation.

There is an old Jamaican story told of a man who had reached the bottom and decided to end it all. He climbed a tree and, as he sat there waiting for the right moment to jump, he ate his last meal of a ripe banana and dropped the skin on the ground. As he was about to jump, another man wandered under the tree and, seeing the banana peel, started to eat it.

The man hurriedly decided not to jump and went back home. He had realised that as bad as his life was there were others that were worse off. That moment became his phoenix point.

Your phoenix point may not even happen during a low point in life. It may come when you realise that the friends you have will not help you to accomplish your dreams; you need to move and leave them behind. You may be sitting an exam and realise you need to work harder for that scholarship.

A phoenix point is when you realise there needs to be some change and you start working to bring about that change. Recognise YOUR phoenix point and start moving.

CHAPTER 23

The Cage

'Mommy! Mommy! Wake up! It's my school trip day. Wake up pleeeease! Today we are going to the zoo and we are going to see horses and kangaroos and bears and lions and all the animals in the world. Mom wake up!'

'Charlie, why on earth do you never call your daddy?' I groaned and rolled over pulling the pillow over my head. With my eyes still covered I reached blindly but instinctively for the bedside table, searching for my phone to check the time. After feeling around for a few seconds I felt my phone and drew it under the pillow where my eyes could see the time. '5am,' I groaned.

'Wake up Sam,' I kicked him under the sheet, 'Charlie is talking to you. Wake up!' He barely moved and just a muffled sound escaped his lips. 'Men,' I groaned. I was too tired to even attempt to take Charlie back to his bed. I just eased over, pillow still firmly held over my head. Charlie snuggled into the space created and immediately positioned his bony knees in the curve of my back. For Christmas I am getting a lock for my bedroom door I thought.

After several minutes of twisting and turning we all finally settled into a comfortable position and drifted off to sleep.

Five minutes later it was 7am and the alarms started blaring. I could tell it was going to be one of those days. Yep, half-way through eating burnt toast, wiping the coffee stains from my new top and searching desperately for my car keys my theory was holding up. I gave up on the keys and Sam agreed to drop us off.

Finally we all made it to the car, to my surprise fully dressed, packed lunches in hand and heading in the right direction.

Sam pulled up at the school gate and I immediately felt a strong dislike for whoever made the new rule that a parent should accompany under-sixes on public trips. Why could I not have become pregnant one year earlier? Too late now I grimaced, grabbed our lunches and headed into the school with Charlie chattering excitedly next to me.

About half an hour of fluffing around and doing a million head counts, we were finally off. After one thousand questions from Charlie and his mates, sick on my shoes and several rounds of the wheels on the bus I was not holding out much hope for any improvements. Yep, my theory was still holding up. I hoped Sam slipped on a banana peel. Well what do you know, always an exception to the rule, one pleasant thought so far I smiled.

Finally we arrived at the zoo. At last it was time to see some animals that walk on four feet and live in cages. We walked around and enjoyed looking at all the animals and even feeding some of them. After about an hour Charlie and I wandered away from the group desperate for a little peace and quiet and quality time. We took a small path that went under some bushes. We came upon a cage where we could see a huge black bear pacing back and forth. It only took him seconds to walk from one end of his cage to the other. His pacing seemed futile as I am sure if he stretched himself he could touch both ends easily but still he continued. He saw or smelled us and turned in our direction knocking over a plate of food. Startled, we instinctively stepped backwards. He looked at us; then turned abruptly knocking into the fence.

'Why is he knocking into everything?' Charlie asked looking into my eyes and noticing my tears.

I bent down hugged Charlie tightly and explained 'Son, his cage is too small.'

Final Comments

Are you in a situation where everything you do seems to irritate someone? Even your "Good morning!" seems to upset people. You cannot do any good no matter how hard you try. Everywhere you turn you are perceived to be causing some trouble. You are working extra hard but everyone else is getting promoted and you are feeling frustrated.

Maybe … just maybe, your cage is too small.

You may need to widen your boundaries by getting to know more people that appreciate you for who you are. Possibly start looking for another job where your efforts will be valued. Never limit yourself to your current situation; the world is a big place. Do not build your cage so small you cannot move. Extend your boundaries and experience new things to grow your expectations and perspectives.

I have always been puzzled when long service awards are given to people for being in the same job for over thirty years. Now before I lose people here, allow me to explain. I can understand someone starting in one position and changing job roles and getting promoted over the years. They may have been in the same company for all those years but they have actually moved; changed locations or job descriptions.

My bewilderment is for people who have remained in the same position for over thirty years doing the same job. They have created a small cage because it felt comfortable and offered security and minimal risks. What a limitation to place on yourself.

Do not limit your potential. Be all you were created to be. Les Brown, noted motivational speaker once said we should all "Live full and die empty."

CHAPTER 24

The Thief

'He's coming, he's coming!' Mark whispered nervously switching from one leg to the next. For a moment he reminded me of a little child desperate to use the toilet.

'I'll delay him while you guys search the place,' Tony suggested.

'Go ahead. We'll whistle when we are done,' I replied.

Tony quickly exited via the side door we had used to gain entry earlier. As soon as he was outside we started searching frantically, conscious that we had very little time. The first drawer I opened in the study yielded six gold watches. 'Kerching!' I whispered and waved my discovery for Mark to see.

In the second drawer I found a huge wad of cash, at least $20 000. That was the most money I had ever seen in real life. I kissed it and hurriedly placed it in my coat pocket. 'Mark?' I whispered, 'Where are you?'

'Come here, George,' he whispered and I could sense the urgency in his voice. Quickly I rushed to the room he was in. I opened the door and stood with my mouth wide open in disbelief; putting my hands over my mouth in fear any sound should escape. We stood staring into certain early retirement as inside the little room attached to the study stood an open safe full of diamonds.

'Mother of glory!' I finally managed to whisper, my hand now atop my head.

A few seconds after the initial shock had worn off, greed quickly took over. We hurriedly stuffed every pocket and space we could find on our person. We were rich, very, very rich. We could not wipe the grins off our faces. Our days as small-time crooks were finally over; we had struck the big lottery.

After we had packed all we could carry we slowly tip-toed to the window at the front of the house. We could see Tony busily chatting to the old man. I was just about to place two fingers in my mouth to give the signal whistle when I heard a low almost inaudible sound. I quickly looked at Mark to check if he had heard the sound too. His panicked expression confirmed my fears.

We slowly turned towards the stairs and putting my index finger to my lips we froze to listen but could hear nothing. Mid-way through turning back to the window, from somewhere upstairs the sound came again, a low painful groan. We looked at each other puzzled. 'I thought the house was empty?' I whispered. We had been staking out the house for months and we knew the old man lived alone. The housekeeper only came on Monday, Wednesday and Friday. Today was Thursday.

'Me too.' Mark replied.

We slowly tiptoed in the direction of the stairs walking towards the sound. We crept up the stairs and came to a door that was slightly ajar; I pushed the door open so we could have a peek inside.

Lying on a bed in the centre of the room was a woman. She looked like death itself. Her skin was pale, her eyes sunken and all her hair completely gone; the only sign of life was the low groan of pain that escaped her mouth. 'Dad,' she moaned. Slowly we closed the door and stepped back outside the room. Neither of us said a word, just exchanged a look of pity and a shake of the head.

We quietly retreated back to the window where we could see Tony and gave a low whistle. Tony glanced in our direction, quickly gave the old man a gentle slap on the back and jogged off towards the waiting car as we made our way through the side door.

The old man looked at Tony with bewilderment. You could see he was slightly irritated to be delayed, but Mr Marron was glad to help a lost young man. The old man walked as quickly as his frail legs would allow him towards his house. He opened his door and entered, noticing in his peripheral vision that the door to his office was slightly ajar; he thought it was strange but he was more preoccupied with getting to his cancer stricken daughter upstairs. He had rushed out to the book store to purchase her favourite storybook, *The Day Time Stood Still*. He gently touched the bedroom door handle and pushed it ajar. He saw her chest heave then slowly came down and never rise again.

The three men in the car heard the piercing scream; thought their crime was discovered and hurriedly drove off. The driver was momentarily distracted and drove straight into the back of a police car.

§

The old man slowly dragged himself to the front door. He had been trying to ignore the persistent ringing of the doorbell for the past ten minutes, hoping whoever it was would go away. He was greeted by the lost jogger, two other strangers and two police officers. As the police explained the situation the old man looked at all three men with deep sadness and pain in his eyes.

'Would you like to press charges sir?' the officer enquired for the second time as the old man slowly tried to mentally process the scene that was unfolding before him.

The man hung his head as if lost in thoughts for a while. Slowly he lifted his old tired head, 'Yes, but only against one man. These two men,' he said, pointing at myself and Mark, 'I give the jewellery, the money, watches and diamonds you found on them because I no longer have any use for them. My precious daughter died today and they were her inheritance. But this

106

man,' he pointed a bony finger at Tony, 'this man I want to be prosecuted to the full extent of the law because he's the worst of all thieves. I will spend the rest of my fortune to make sure he rots behind bars,' he spoke with strength and conviction.

'B-B-ut!' Tony exclaimed. He was puzzled and bewildered as the police officers dragged him off.

We lingered in disbelief, afraid to move from the spot; stood as if rooted to the doorstep. We nervously looked from Tony to the old man, back to Tony again, and then back again to the old man.

Bravely Mark finally asked the obvious question, 'W-what? W-why? How...?'

The old man looked at us with tears and lost hope clearly visible in his eyes and replied.

'You stole things I could replace, but your friend took my time and so my daughter died alone.'

He quietly turned and closed his door.

We stood silently for a while staring at the closed door. Slowly we emptied our pockets of everything we had stolen and left them at the door. We turned and slowly walked away.

Final Comments

It has always amazed me how people treat the greatest asset they own and how carelessly they allow others to use and abuse it. Most people will spend huge fortunes to protect their material wealth but are reckless with their use of time. They invest time with people who show no real appreciation or allow their time to be wasted with idle chatter, gossip, hours watching television or on the telephone just talking about any and every irrelevant thing.

Try this for me please. The next time someone asks you, 'do you have a minute?' Answer with a 'no' and note their reaction. Most people are quite taken aback if you tell them no, even complete strangers feel they have a right to demand a minute from your limited time on earth.

As in the story of *The Thief*, regardless of whatever material things you lose or are stolen from you, you must always remember they can be replaced. The thing that you must always be conscious of is your time.

People will steal your time without you even realising it. These are the worst kind of thieves as they are stealing your most priceless possession, one you will never be able to replace. Time lost cannot be retrieved. Write off what you have already lost but be careful with what is left; most importantly since no one knows exactly how much they have left.

Be careful with your most valuable possession. Beware the thieves of time.

CHAPTER 25

The Machine

'ggjjdddvh@' ggjtu;/. 'hc,gdd'cg hfd.'

'piyrtxgfxczxxcxcx' hhhhhhhhhhhhh.'

'hola, como estas?'

'bonjour?'

'hello?'

'Yes! Yes! Use that setting. It seems this is the language most humans on this piece of land understand,' Blorrd said.

'It is called English. Now remember, we only have fifty minutes on this planet then we must leave before they discover us,' Blorrd reminded his fellow travellers.

'Will we be able to come back?' First Command asked.

'No, never,' Blorrd answered. He was the Senior General for this mission.

'But how will we get our machines back?' Second Command queried.

'Listen, I have always been the brain of this command so let me do the thinking, okay?' Blorrd snapped.

'This is how we do it. Humans are very simple creatures from what I have observed. They all follow certain patterns with very slight deviations. For example, look over there.' He pointed in the direction of southwest.

'Where?' First Command asked. Blorrd shook his head with mild irritation.

'Look there,' he pointed again. 'Look at that human in the white top. Can you see her?'

Both Commanders nodded in the affirmative.

'She works at Point A but she has taken the same route every day for the past five years. She only takes a different route when there is a road closure. She even sits in traffic never trying to figure out an alternative route. She listens to the same radio station every morning. She shops at the same supermarket and usually buys the same items even though there are thousands of other items there. Set patterns - they feel comfortable in the same routine,' Blorrd explained.

'Look over here now. I bet I can guess which coffee that guy orders. Over thirty-four choices but every morning the same one, latte! Sits in the same corner and reads the same newspaper. A whole world and they create tiny bubbles to live in. We definitely picked the right place,' he concluded.

'Now here is the plan. We will hide these machines inside the humans. Whenever a new human is created, the older human will replicate the machine and embed it inside the new one. I have already attached a tracker device so when the human expires the machine will find itself back to our planet undetected by the evil Magorda. It's the most brilliant plan ever.'

Magorda was the evil one from the nearby planet of Graet and wanted their machines to create his own army. He realised their power and had been searching for the last century to find them.

'I don't know,' First Command said.

'It's fool-proof. What could go wrong?' Blorrd asked.

'What if the humans discover this machine? It's way too powerful for them. They could actually start breaking their usual patterns and do extraordinary things that would cause the other humans to detect there was something different about that one. Then what?' added Second Command.

'Trust me, I have lived amongst human beings for a long while just observing and ninety-nine percent follow some set pattern. They will not know,' Blorrd reassured.

'Well ok. Let us do it and get out of here. We can only hope they remain in ignorance,' Second Command replied.

With that Blorrd pressed the button and in an instant all human beings were implanted with the machine.

§

Centuries later, from a distant galaxy far, far away, a silent alarm went off at headquarters.

First Command whispered to the panic-stricken generals as they rushed into headquarters. 'Look! Look at that human without a shirt; he is not following his usual pattern anymore.'

All the generals leaned over to get a closer look at the screen.

'He is standing up straighter and walking with a purpose. It is as if he knows something that the others do not yet know.'

'Oh my God he has just fired his boss and ordered an espresso!'

'Fool proof eh!? shffyjcvcjgddj g ...' First Command screamed.

'English please!' the senior General requested. 'Is there any proof he knows?'

'Yes sir! This human has discovered the implanted machine, sir. There are very high levels of activity; he is actually thinking, sir! We do not know how long before others discover theirs too.'

Everyone sat, transfixed to see what would happen next.

Final Comments

Buried deep inside every one of us is an infinite source of power waiting to be discovered and used; it is called the mind.

Most people have stopped thinking. Yes we have thoughts but only superficial ones like, 'what shall we cook for dinner?' or, 'did I get a text?' or, 'I hate my job.' But many do not go beyond that. They do not think about the implications of eating certain things for dinner; the effect on their bodies. Or what quantities to cook to reduce waste and give the correct portion sizes. No thought about whether the meal is balanced and how it will appear on the plate. We just limit ourselves to what I call "surface thoughts". We need to recognise the power inside us and start using it.

Some people are born, exist, then die. They have failed to leave any mark on this world. Others need to know you were here and remember you when you are gone. You may not become a President or a movie star but whatever you decide to be; be the very best you can. My neighbour loves to garden and has created the most beautiful garden in our neighbourhood that we all talk about regularly and stop to admire. She is being the best at what she does. She will be remembered.

One of the worst things we do is to allow others to think for us. We are told what to do, where to sit and what to wear and never ask, 'why?' Instead we sometimes choose to blindly follow.

Are you using your mind to the fullest? Have you found the machine buried deep inside you? Start looking for it today, it is there. Find it and start directing your own life instead of being directed by others. Discover something new today. Break the mould and realise your true potential.

CHAPTER 26

How Much Weight Can You Carry?

In a land far, far away; much, much further than that! There existed two beautiful kingdoms each ruled by a kind and loving monarch.

The Jems lived on a high mountain top and would spend their days farming because that is what they enjoyed. The Jems were ruled by Queen Cilda and were very happy people.

On the neighbouring mountain lived the Vods and they spent their days making huge machines because that is what they enjoyed. The Vods were ruled by King Dan and they all loved him for he was a kind and gentle ruler.

Once every year both kingdoms would meet in the valley between and celebrate together for they were friendly kingdoms. They would have loved to meet more often but it took almost four months to trek down to the valley and four months back up to the top. The other four months were spent enjoying what their work and preparing for the festival of celebration.

§

Today was the opening of the tenth annual festival and both kingdoms were excited to start the festivities. Both king and queen cut the ribbon and the festivities were declared open. It was a magical time. There was music, dancing, food and many types of entertainment and entertainers. It was certainly a wonderful place to be.

The two monarchs sat side by side on their thrones watching and swaying to the beats of the music and dining on some exotic fruits grown in the valley between both kingdoms. Both were now getting old and preferred to sit and watch, allowing the younger folk to enjoy the festivities.

'You know,' Queen Cilda said to King Dan, 'Wouldn't it be a great idea if we could somehow meet more often?'

'It certainly would,' King Dan replied, 'but the journey is too long and tiresome. It would be impossible to coordinate so many activities and trek up and down these mountains any faster.'

The queen nodded in agreement and focussed her attention on the young men playing at a coconut shy in the far corner of the field. A young lady sitting nearby had heard the conversation between the two monarchs and was eager to make a contribution, as she had thought the very same thing. She belonged to the kingdom of the Jems and had fallen in love with a man who lived in the kingdom of Vods. She desperately wished they could meet more often than once every year, so bravely she cleared her throat and requested permission to speak.

'Permission granted,' Queen Cilda responded.

'Ma'am, why don't we build a connection between the two mountains? It would shorten the journey to just days or hours and we could visit the other kingdom more than just once a year.'

Both monarchs were silent for a while then King Dan responded, 'that is a brilliant idea. Is it possible?'

A quick nod from the young lady confirmed that it could actually be done.

'We shall do it immediately,' Queen Cilda chimed in.

§

The best engineers from both kingdoms started working almost immediately on designing a new bridge to join the two kingdoms. After many moons they finally settled on a design and once it was approved by the monarchs, started to construct the bridge.

Within three years they had completed a shiny new bridge. Excitedly both monarchs cut the ribbon and each declared the bridge open at their end. The queen nervously made her way across the bridge first and was met at the centre by King Dan. They exchanged pleasantries and flipped a turtle to decide where the first celebrations would be held. 'Heads,' called king Dan just as the turtle landed with his head up. With a smile both monarchs walked hand in hand towards the kingdom of Vods.

With great excitement and anticipation the kingdoms let out a huge cheer and everyone from the kingdom of Jems rushed on to the bridge eager to get to the other side. Most of the people from Jems were already mid-way over the bridge when they heard the first ominous creak. Everyone stopped to listen ... then they heard another loud creak and the bridge started shaking. The horror on their faces reflected the realisation of their fatal mistake. Everyone started running towards a kingdom but tragedy struck and the bridge gave way. All those on the bridge plummeted to their deaths.

The design was flawed; it could not hold up under the weight of so many people at once.

Both kingdoms declared ten years of mourning to remember their lost friends and family.

Final Comments

How much can you take before you break? This is information you need to know before it is too late.

Everyone needs to do a SWOT analysis to identify your Strengths and Weaknesses, prepare for your Opportunities and be aware of the Threats that may come. Do not just sit idly by waiting until that moment in life comes when you realise that you cannot make it; you are going to break. It may be too late; you may not have all the support in place to help you hold all that weight.

You know that your job is your life; it defines you but you are not working for yourself. You need to make sure you know what to do if the business should close, go bankrupt or you are made redundant. Do you have a plan B? You should know the business strategy of your workplace whether you are just a cleaner or a branch manager. The CEO might decide to merge branches to create a more efficient business module. Will you be chosen as the new manager? What new skills have you acquired since you have been in this job or have you just relaxed and sat waiting for your Christmas bonus and retirement?

If you are the cleaner have they invented some new machines that will eliminate the need for so many cleaners? Will they decide to use college kids instead of people over forty? Will you be able to take that weight?

On an emotional level, how much does your partner support you? Although it is not a thought we like to have ... what if? Without planning for the worst (as thoughts can become self-fulfilling) you need to prepare yourself for those unexpected bumps in the road called life. Would you be able to cope emotionally, mentally, financially? How much would it take to break you?

It is your responsibility to analyse your life at least once a month and know your breaking point; start now to put the support in place while you are busy living. God, family and true friends are the strongest support I know of. Yours might be different or more extensive, it does not matter as long as they are in place before that testing weight presents itself.

Know your breaking point!

CHAPTER 27

Complete the Sentences

Mrs Matthews was my favourite teacher up until this point. I had even bought her some expensive chocolate to give to her today as it was the last day of the Christmas term. But I had changed my mind; I decided to eat every single piece of chocolate with my friends. Which teacher decides to give a test on the last day?

I hated her.

'Put all your books away. Pens, erasers and pencils on your desks please because today you have your English end of term test. You will be getting five sentences and you must complete each sentence using the appropriate words of your choice. Please check all punctuation and ensure each letter is formed correctly.'

'Remember:

- A sentence must express a complete thought.
- It must begin with a capital letter and end with a full stop.
- All sentences must have a noun and a finite verb.'

'You have twenty minutes.'

This may have sounded easy but I assure you, being born in Japan and speaking Japanese for the first fourteen of my fourteen and a half years meant that completing this test was one of the hardest challenges I had faced since being enrolled in an English speaking school by my parents. I do not know why on earth I needed to speak English anyway.

- The dog and the bear ....
- .... ran to the shops
- When will..
- Yesterday I was ....
- I am ....

Final Comments

How did you complete sentence number 5?

Was your answer based on someone else's view of you? Did you answer based on your current mood? Did you answer based on a label or a category you were placed in at birth? Did you answer using your relationship to others, your job or ...?

Were you a mother, sister, good friend, happy, doctor, lawyer, man, woman, child?

Is that really YOU?

This is one of the simplest but most difficult questions. It is easy to answer if answered in haste but with deeper thinking it is clear that whatever words you chose that is essentially how you define yourself. Too often without any thought we allow others to define us and put us in categories where we may not belong. You need to write your own label and description; tell people who you are and do not allow others to tell you who you are.

We define ourselves based on our relationship to others and our positions in life. Try not to define yourself based on other's labels or positions. This does not represent your essence.

Find a quiet place, close your eyes for about ten minutes and think about that question. Now go back and answer that question with conviction.

In the Bible when Moses asked the Lord, 'who are you?'

The lord himself replied, 'I am that I am.'

He was so much more that words could not describe or complete the sentence.

We know that words are self-fulfilling so be very careful how you decide to complete question number 5.

CHAPTER 28

Walk in My shoes

'196...197...198...199! Wow! 199 pairs of shoes? You do realise you need help and very soon.' Mom sternly warned.

'I know, I know,' I sheepishly replied secretly thinking; just one more pair and I would have 200.

'Let's put them away quickly before James and my sons come home. They would never understand. Men!' I shrugged.

'That is very sexist,' said Mom as she perched her glasses half-way down her nose to add emphasis to her glare.

'Ok, ok, my men would not understand,' I answered, rolling my eyes as soon as she glanced away.

'I saw that,' she replied quickly, as she unexpectedly turned her head back in my direction. 'I know you by now. I only brought you into this world and watched you grow into a shoe addict,' she quipped.

My mother always had to get the final word but I would not exchange her for the world.

We had boxed and stashed shoes for about half an hour when we heard the sound of a car engine coming from outside followed by the front door opening.

'Honey I'm home,' my husband shouted from downstairs.

'Coming love,' I answered.

'Mom leave the shoes and let's go,' I hurriedly went downstairs and was greeted by an open pair of arms, a complaint, a shake of the head and a grunt.

As I hugged my husband James, Tendayi started to complain that his brother Alexander was being mean all the way home; Alex shrugged his shoulders, rolled his eyes and shook his head while my seventeen year old Anthony just grunted and ran up the stairs eager to get away from the noise. He was not being rude nor did he have any strong dislike for us but his Asperger's meant he hated loud noises.

I patted Anthony on the shoulder as he pushed past and was rewarded with a whisper, 'I love you Mommy,' I smiled.

'Ok! Ok! Grandma is here,' Mom announced herself once she had reached the bottom of the stairs. 'Give me some love,' she beckoned to Tendayi and Alex. They rushed into her arms. They all loved Grandma Bertha.

'Now go on upstairs and change your clothes. I have already cooked your favourite,' she chided.

'None of that West Indian chicken though,' Alex shot back as he ran up the stairs with Tendayi in hot pursuit.

Within ten minutes both Alex and Tendayi were in the kitchen ready to devour whatever Grandma Bertha had prepared. Alex was just about to peek in the pot on the cooker and had lifted the lid to discover what Grandma had cooked when my scream caused him to drop the lid, making quite a loud noise. The noise startled Grandma who turned around too quickly and knocked the tomato sauce off the edge of the counter right onto Tendayi's feet who was standing just behind her.

Tendayi stood still and did not flinch for two reasons. First the noise and the open mouths of everyone were causing him some alarm. Second, he knew the reason behind the scream that had come from deep inside my throat. So he stood there, looking at me, afraid to break eye contact just in case I did something horrible when his back was turned.

'What was that scream?' James cried as he rushed into the kitchen followed by Anthony. No one answered, they could not and no one moved.

Conscious that everyone was staring at me, and realising I may have overreacted and anticipating the barrage of judgemental statements that would greet me in a few minutes, I gently closed my eyes and pointed in the direction of the source of my pain and sudden outburst. Tendayi immediately started crying, almost as loudly as someone sentenced to the gallows.

His wails escalated to a crescendo as all eyes turned in the direction of my fingers, passed Alex, past the stool past the cooker and came to rest on the feet of Tendayi.

Tendayi stood still. His shirt and trousers were covered in tomato sauce but he did not mind that too much. Slowly his eyes drifted down to join the other pairs of eyes which were all focussed on his feet which were also swimming in tomato sauce.

Tendayi stood bawling because on his feet were the broken white (well red) suede shoes I had just bought today.

Through his sobs we could barely make out the muffled words, 'Mommy, I just wanted to walk in your shoes.'

Final Comments

What does it mean to walk in somebody's shoes?

Did you know an average woman buys four pairs of new shoes every year? Not a particularly startling fact but for me it adds a little bit of substance to the fact that I have always believed myself to be extraordinary or above average because I buy at least eight pairs of shoes per year.

Now you might be sitting there thinking she has a problem or an addiction but let me assure you I do not. Shoes have always been my passion and everywhere I go I am always complimented or questioned regarding my taste in shoes. I have even gone into schools where children stop to look under the desk to see what shoes I am wearing; their compliments are usually greeted with a smile and thank you and I just move along.

But there was one particular girl who stopped me in the corridor quite aggressively and said, 'miss, how many shoes you have?' I smiled and tried to avoid answering the question by saying, 'I really don't know.'

She persisted, 'what size are you?'

I said 'I'm a size six,' to which she responded gleefully, 'so am I,' and then she said flippantly, 'miss I would love to walk in your shoes.'

On any ordinary day I would have walked on and not thought too much about that comment, but then it struck me. Did she understand what it meant to be walking in my shoes? I think not.

For example; did she know that I was born years ago to a very poor family in Jamaica? That I only owned one pair of shoes and those shoes had to take me to church, any special occasion, school and occasionally running over the neighbour's house. Did she know I walked in plastic shoes for five years and when the sun heated those shoes you could actually feel the heat going through your body? Did she know the pain I felt? Did she know there was a gas strike in 1988 and I had to walk over twenty miles just to reach home in those plastic shoes? Did she know how many journeys I have taken wearing those shoes just to get were I am standing today?

She did not, but her question resonated with me and caused me to reflect briefly on what journeys I have made in my shoes and how easy it is for us sometimes to forget that everybody is walking in their own pair of shoes; completing their own journeys in life. How many times do we stop to admire the style of someone's shoes, the colour, the design, the current state of wear or the brand?

Shoes represent movement, they offer protection for your feet as you move about and, especially for ladies, they are one of the most noticed accessories you will ever wear. If your shoes could talk, what would they say? But since they cannot speak let your stance and gait tell of your journey; walk boldly and confidently. Each morning when you take that first step outside to start your day, think about what you will be doing, where you will be going and step out in confidence to face your day.

CHAPTER 29

The Small Box

It was the most elaborate room I have ever been in. It was difficult to find the right words to describe it. My limited vocabulary would not do it any justice. 'Wow,' is the only word that could escape my lips followed by a sharp inhalation of breath and another whispered, 'wow.'

At the other end of the phone I could hear my Mom asking my Dad, 'What is it like? What is it like?'

'Mom,' I responded, pulling the phone from Dad's hands after being jolted back into reality. 'It's almost indescribable,' I said in complete awe.

'Try anyway,' came my mother's anxious response. Although no one could ever shut my mother up I almost wished she was standing next to me; certain that the magnificence and grandeur would at least silence her for a few minutes.

'The ceilings are so high that you could throw a small child as high as you can without fear of bumping their heads. You would be blinded if you looked up because of all the lights from the many chandeliers glittering like stars above. The walls are painted in white but as you walk past it's like other colours are there as you can catch shades of blue, pastels and red from your peripheral field of vision,

'The windows are framed in elaborate gold designs and are taller than Dad. There are so many I can't count. The carpet under my feet is thick and soft, I am almost tempted to lie down and rub my cheeks against it. With each step I can feel my feet sinking deeper into its plushness. Mom it's absolutely amazing,

'At the far end is one of my favourite rides; the one where you put the money in and pretend to drive. There is a candyfloss machine and through another window I can see great big Lego blocks. There are lots of children playing.'

Dad quickly took the phone which allowed me to catch my breath for a minute. I peeked through the window where the children were busily playing outside. I smiled and they beckoned me over. Dad read my mind before I even asked and shook his head; the happy children belonged on the outside because their parents only worked here. They were not part of the posh people who played inside.

Dad and Mom had recently separated and I had come to spend the Easter break with my dad, an army man. Dad moved around a lot so each holiday brought new places, new people and new friends. Making new friends was always the hardest. We were by no means wealthy but we could afford more than most. I had big dreams; I wanted to become someone famous which always made my Dad smile. I loved when he smiled. Maybe one day Mom will fall in love with that smile again. It is hard being an only child and having your parents break up at ten but I was determined to be brave and enjoy my life. There were certain perks after all from having two parents who compete for your affection. One major perk is that Dad has now been elevated to the status of eligible bachelor which meant women constantly vying for his affections.

Last week Dad and I were invited to one of the poshest parties in town by Miss Flemstead in a bid, I suspect, to lure him into marriage number two. We dressed up in our finest clothes and arrived at the Rogers' huge mansion at the end of a long driveway. After what seemed like hours of smiling and polite, boring conversation, Mrs Rogers mentioned that all the kids met up at a type of clubhouse at the golf club known as Barking Lodge. It was meant to be a fun group, like a kind of treehouse club. She said it might be a good idea if I went and met some children my own age. I was really excited and got up early this morning, dressed in my favourite dress. Dad had taken me to Barking Lodge in his new car. I think to fit in with the setting.

'Can I help you?' a man wandered over and stood next to Dad interrupting my thoughts. He looked like he had been starched from the neck down and dressed like a penguin.

'We were invited by the Rogers' for Cindy here to play with the club-house children,' Dad replied and automatically stood as if he was starched too.

'Ah yes!' Starchy replied, 'We were expecting you,' he pointed to a small door at the far end of the lounge and with a bit of difficulty bent down to tell me I could go straight there and knock. Then he told dad he was welcome to wait in the lounge and have drinks and canapés on the house.

'Thank you,' Dad replied and starchy was off. Dad knelt down so he could see into my eyes, 'will you be okay?' he asked.

'I am fine,' I replied. I was so excited to see what was behind that door. Dad gently kissed my forehead and we went off in separate directions. I knew he was watching so I waved without looking back. I could hear his soft chuckle.

I walked towards the small door, drew a deep breath then knocked. After a few seconds the door was opened by a boy who looked about twelve years old. His skin was much lighter and he had very blue mesmerising eyes. 'I am Cindy. Mrs Rogers said I could come over today,' I informed him.

'Hold on,' he said and shouted for someone named Carlie. Almost immediately a beautifully dressed young girl of about ten appeared at the door.

'My name is Carlie Rogers, can I help?' she said with perfect pronunciation.

'Your Mom told me to come,' I replied, my voice starting to squeak unexpectedly. I felt thirsty, hot and bothered for no reason. My throat felt a bit dry and I shoved my hands into my pockets to hide my nervousness. I turned to find Dad but he had already gone. I slowly turned back to face Carlie just as she was giving me a full body scan. I smiled nervously, she did not.

'I am sorry Mindy but...'

'Cindy,' I corrected, cutting her off mid-sentence and realised my mistake a bit too late. Carlie's face tensed and her gaze narrowed just slightly enough for me to curl my toes in my shoes.

'Yes,' she said, once again giving me a fill body scan and for added effect she paused then continued, 'Cindy,' she drooled, 'my Mom does that kind of thing frequently. She invites every stray she meets, I suppose to be charitable, but this is an exclusive club house. We have no more space. Sorry!' then she slammed the door shut.

I had to blink about three times to see if I was dreaming or if it was just a cruel prank. As the truth became clear tears welled up in my eyes and I turned so quickly I did not realise someone was behind me. I bumped right into starchy who must have quietly crept up behind me. He blocked my escape, leaned over me and knocked at the door then promptly opened it without waiting for a reply. He grabbed me by my hand and half dragged me behind him until we were inside the room.

The room was much tinier than I had imagined. There were about six kids sitting on an old sofa drinking snowballs made from a machine in the corner and listening to music from the radio. 'Look here Miss Carlie Rogers, this girl is staying, like it or not.' Starchy stated with as much authority as he could muster.

I tugged gently on starchy's uniform. 'Never mind,' I whispered, 'I don't want to stay to be honest.' I was eager to go having seen inside; somewhat grateful they did not want me either. The room might have seemed the place to be but I knew outside had more to offer.

Final Comments

As human beings we all like to feel like we belong, sometimes to our own detriment. We feel hurt when we are excluded or barred from somewhere. We convince ourselves that wherever or whatever we are excluded from is the place we must be.

We need to stop sometimes and look at the bigger picture.

I was working at school years ago and became *persona non grata* because I did not follow the (m)asses. I remember going in to drop off a package at the front gate and a very senior figure completely ignored my presence even after ringing that buzzer multiple times. She walked around in that tiny glass box called reception without acknowledging my presence.

Now in her small mind I can bet she was thinking "I am so important, I will let her stand there and wait. She is insignificant and I don't want her inside this place."

But the truth is, in my mind I was thinking, 'she thinks she is locking me out of this small box but does not realise that she is actually locking herself inside. There is a world open behind me'. I felt pity rather than hatred at that time to be honest. In her limited understanding of life she thought she was hurting me because she was inside a small box and did not want me to come inside to join her in her small box.

I smiled and walked back outside into a bigger, better and more beautiful world where there were no walls and no glass boxes. Today I am grateful she locked me out. Letting me in would have prevented me from achieving my dreams.

CHAPTER 30

The Escalator

'Let's go! We're late,' I cried out in exasperation.

'One more time please, just one more time,' Cynthia cajoled and quickly dashed off before I could even offer a reply. I stood watching their heads slowly going down until they were completely out of sight. I did not move from my spot; I stood there waiting. For the past half an hour I had been standing in the same spot waiting for them to ride the escalator up and down. I could see the strange looks they received each time they went up and down again so I had chosen to stand at a discrete distance so no one would know we were together.

After about ten seconds their heads slowly reappeared.

'You've got to see this,' Margaret said, excitedly grabbing me by both arms and propelling me forward. After physically and verbally trying to protest, I finally relented and went with my two besties.

'We were meant to be shopping, girls,' I said trying to reason with whatever shreds of common sense remained.

'We know, but look at this! Look at the picture in that store on floor two, what do you see?' bestie number one, Cynthia asked.

'A really, really hot guy advertising cologne and I must admit, it is a rather nice poster,' I agreed. 'Now can we please go?'

'His face,' bestie number two Margaret chirped in.

'Well, he is looking sad and kind of grumpy,' I replied. Strange for a poster I thought.

'Yep,' bestie number one agreed, 'now let's get on the escalator and keep looking at the billboard ad.' slowly we descended. 'Look now,' she squealed, 'notice anything new?' I could clearly see the change and a wry smile crept to the corners of my mouth. At eye level, sure enough the hot guy on the poster seemed to have lost his frown and now he looked as if he was neither smiling nor frowning. He was just looking at us with no expression on his face.

We were still not finished I surmised by the glint in their eyes. 'Just keep looking,' Margaret said, 'Wait for it.'

'Oh my gosh!' I covered my mouth to quiet my outburst. From the ground floor, just below the ad, it seemed as if the guy was now smiling. Clearly an optical illusion I concluded with obvious admiration. That is so funny.

Bestie number one said, 'I told you: you can see different things depending on where you stand looking at the very same picture. Hilarious.'

'Let's go up again!' I begged.

Final Comments

There are times in life when you feel a person has been sent by God himself to rescue you from some dire and disastrous situation and you sing his or her praise every day. You speak constantly about the person's good graces and you pledge eternal gratitude.

That person may have helped you financially, physically, emotionally or even spiritually. And slowly you start believing, using and relying on that help to better yourself and you start to rise up, out of your current situation. You can start to see visible changes in your life. A new job or promotion, a new car, maybe a new relationship or a change in your living situation or you have studied and gained more qualifications and progressed to some new heights.

But as your circumstances improve you may eventually find yourself on the same level as your helper and you might start noticing that the big wide smile is no longer there, just a blank expression and you cannot understand the change. The person may now start to make excuses about meeting up or can no longer offer the same level of help they had originally promised.

Still grateful and motivated you keep pushing to higher heights. You may have moved onto a better geographical location, completed a second degree, bought a newer luxurious car, improved your finances until eventually you are now above the person who used to help you out. This is when you notice the smile is completely gone, the blank expression absent and now replaced by a bitter scowl and you cannot understand why.

Why would someone who you saw as an angel sent from above now seem to despise the ground you walk on?

It is because some people like to help you when you are at the bottom. They get a certain satisfaction from looking down on people. They are glad to help, but do not like it when you rise above them. They like to hand you a slice of bread instead of teaching you to bake for yourself. Some people like to help so the world can see their good works and heap praises on their heads but they prefer it if you remain in need.

You need to be able to recognise the help you are getting and act accordingly.

About the Author

V. F. Hoffman-Jackson was born in Jamaica but she has lived in the UK for the past twelve years. She has worked in the educational sector for over twenty years in various leadership roles and has been consistently judged as an outstanding classroom practitioner. She enjoys reading, writing and the occasional game of chess. She is a multi-award-winning motivational speaker and regularly writes motivational articles published in magazines such as Blackbright News. She is the single mother of three boys and considers her role as mom the most important thing in life. Vinette worships at Miracle COGIC in Bedford.

Printed in Great Britain
by Amazon